DIRECT HITS

Essential
Vocabulary

First Edition

For more information, please contact us by mail:

Direct Hits Publishing
2 The Prado, Unit 2, Atlanta GA 30309

Ted@DirectHitsPublishing.com

Or visit our website:
www.DirectHitsPublishing.com

First Edition: April 2016

Despite our best efforts at editing and proofreading, the book may contain errors. Please feel free to contact us if you find an error, and any corrections can be found on our website.

ISBN: 978-1-936551-20-0

Written by Paget Hines
Edited by Ted Griffith
Cover Design by Carlo da Silva
Interior Design by Alison Rayner

Other Books by Direct Hits

Direct Hits Essential Vocabulary is part of a larger series aimed at helping students improve their vocabulary. The series is designed as a progression to help students learn vocabulary as they get older, starting with *Direct Hits Essential Vocabulary*, then *Direct Hits Core Vocabulary*, and finally *Direct Hits Advanced Vocabulary*. Our books are available from Amazon, Barnes & Nobles, and other major retailers.

For information on bulk orders, please email us at:
Ted@DirectHitsPublishing.com

ACKNOWLEDGEMENTS

This first edition reflects the collaborative efforts of an outstanding team of students, educators, reviewers, and project managers, each committed to helping young people attain their highest aspirations. Their insights and talents have been incorporated into *Direct Hits Essential Vocabulary*.

I wish to express my gratitude to Frances Dickson, learning specialist at the San Francisco Friends School, and Michael Richman, English teacher at New Design High School, who gave feedback on early drafts and helped refine the examples. A special thank you to Molly Foran Yurchak, English teacher at Westridge School, for her diligent and specific edits. Her keen eye and thoughtful observations guided the final draft.

I am grateful to educator Martha Shadle for her valuable insights, gleaned from her tutoring experience and Orton-Gillingham training.

I am incredibly indebted to Jane Armstrong, middle school Bible teacher at The Westminster Schools, for her editing and eloquent wordsmithing. She devoted hours to reading over each page of this book through multiple drafts.

Judy Martinez was vital in the editing process. She combed each page to ensure that the grammar was consistent, and she helped me simplify and condense the examples when needed.

Alison Rayner was responsible for creating our interior design. I thank her not only for her creative talent, but also for her flexibility through multiple revisions. Additionally, I am grateful to Carlo da Silva, who once again used his artistic and graphic skills to design our distinctive cover.

Direct Hits Essential Vocabulary would not be possible without Claire Griffith. Her vision for Direct Hits guided every aspect of this book. A big thank you goes out to Luther Griffith for his oversight and support. I appreciate his strong and practical guidance and organization.

A special thank you to Ted Griffith, who was with me for every step of this book. I could not have asked for a better partner. Many long days were made easier with endless cups of coffee and amusing stories.

Finally, I have to thank my family. Specifically, I am grateful to Tanner Hines, sophomore at The Westminster Schools. His humor and honesty helped me make this book as entertaining and readable for teens as possible. My sweet husband, Adam Savage, enabled me to take the time to write this book. I also appreciate my 4-year-old, Iris Savage, who spent many an hour "working" next to me as I tweaked this book.

Paget Hines, *Author*

TABLE OF CONTENTS

prefix
suffix
root

2–10
5 each

INTRODUCTION

Why is vocabulary important, you ask?

Words are our tools for learning and communicating. A rich and varied vocabulary enables us to…

Speak more eloquently…

Describe more vividly…

Argue more compellingly…

Articulate more precisely…

Write more convincingly.

A powerful and vibrant vocabulary can help students score higher across all subject areas and on standardized tests. Unfortunately, traditional vocabulary study can be a tedious chore as students spend hours and hours memorizing long lists of seemingly random words.

Their frustration is understandable!

Direct Hits Essential Vocabulary offers **a different approach**. Each word is illustrated through relevant examples from popular movies, television, literature, music, science, historical events, and current headlines. Students can place the words in a context they can easily understand and remember.

Direct Hits Essential Vocabulary targets middle school and early high school learners, focusing on words students need to know as part of the Common Core curriculum as well as words frequently found on standardized tests like the SSAT and PSAT. Expanded vocabulary knowledge is addressed in the Pro Tip boxes and the Prefix/Root/Suffix boxes, and each chapter concludes with a review.

Building on the success of the *Core Vocabulary* and *Advanced Vocabulary* books, the authors of *Direct Hits Essential Vocabulary* consulted teachers, tutors, learning specialists, parents, and students to ensure that these words and illustrations are on target to prepare kids for vocabulary success in and out of the classroom.

Direct Hits offers **selective** vocabulary using **relevant** examples with **vivid** presentation so you can achieve successful **results** on standardized tests and in life.

Let's get started!

HOW TO USE THIS BOOK

❶ The vocabulary word is always in bold print and capitalized. Words are listed alphabetically in each chapter.

❷ If a word is starred (✦), then the word is a Common Core Academic Vocabulary aligned word.

❸ This is the word number, not the page number. All of the Direct Hits words are numbered in the order they appear in the Essential, Core, and Advanced books.

❺ When another Direct Hits vocabulary word is used, the word will be in bold print and capitalized. The word number (or book it is from) is inside the parentheses.

❹ The part of speech is capitalized and comes before the definition.

❻ The Pro Tip box is additional information to help expand your vocabulary knowledge.

❼ The example is written to show the vocabulary word in context.

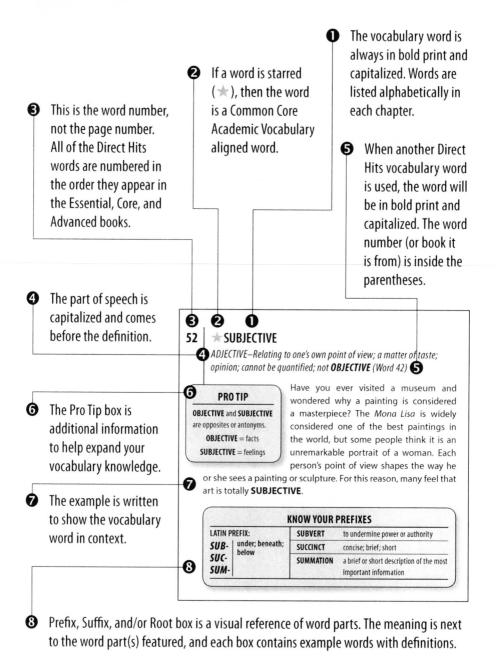

❸ ❷ ❶

52 ✦ SUBJECTIVE

❹ ADJECTIVE—Relating to one's own point of view; a matter of taste; opinion; cannot be quantified; not **OBJECTIVE** (Word 42) **❺**

❻
PRO TIP
OBJECTIVE and **SUBJECTIVE** are opposites or antonyms.
OBJECTIVE = facts
SUBJECTIVE = feelings

Have you ever visited a museum and wondered why a painting is considered a masterpiece? The *Mona Lisa* is widely considered one of the best paintings in the world, but some people think it is an unremarkable portrait of a woman. Each person's point of view shapes the way he or she sees a painting or sculpture. For this reason, many feel that art is totally **SUBJECTIVE**.

❼

KNOW YOUR PREFIXES

LATIN PREFIX:			
SUB-	under; beneath; below	**SUBVERT**	to undermine power or authority
SUC-		**SUCCINCT**	concise; brief; short
SUM-		**SUMMATION**	a brief or short description of the most important information

❽ Prefix, Suffix, and/or Root box is a visual reference of word parts. The meaning is next to the word part(s) featured, and each box contains example words with definitions.

CHAPTER 1

Essential 25 Greatest Hits

Want to be a vocabulary rock star? Look no further than the Essential 25 Greatest Hits. Just like the iTunes and Billboard singles charts, Direct Hits has compiled vocabulary's current Greatest Hits. These are high-frequency words found on academic vocabulary lists like Common Core and recent lower level and upper level SSATs. These 25 words will have you rocking it in no time!

1 | ★AUTHENTIC

ADJECTIVE—Genuine; real; not false or copied

Reality television shows such as *Keeping Up With the Kardashians* claim that they are **AUTHENTIC** portrayals of real life, but these shows are scripted and not as genuine as they appear.

2 | ★BENEFIT

NOUN—Something that is advantageous or good
VERB—To help; to improve; to gain

Doctors regularly point out the **BENEFITS** of daily exercise to their patients, emphasizing that even walking 45 minutes each day can help them stay fit.

Recycling **BENEFITS** the environment because it keeps aluminum cans, among other items, out of landfills and enables them to be processed into new products. A major **BENEFIT** is less waste in landfills.

3 | BENEVOLENT

ADJECTIVE—Characterized by or expressing goodwill or kindly feelings; compassionate

Martin Luther King, Jr. was a **BENEVOLENT** civil rights leader. He preached non-violence as a means of fighting racism and **PREJUDICE** (Word 257). His calls for peaceful change united people of goodwill across the country.

KNOW YOUR PREFIXES		
LATIN PREFIX:	**BENIGN**	gentle; not harmful
BENE- | good	**BENEFACTOR** (Word 215)	a person who makes a gift
	BENEDICTION (DH Core)	bestowing of a blessing

4 | BELLIGERENT

ADJECTIVE—Warlike; given to waging war; aggressively hostile

In *The Hunger Games*, Haymitch Abernathy is the **BELLIGERENT** mentor to Katniss and Peeta. After winning the second Quarter Quell, Haymitch becomes an angry and bitter drunk. When he first meets Katniss and Peeta, Haymitch is hostile and unkind, saying:

"*You've got about as much charm as a dead slug.***"**

5 | ★BIAS

NOUN—A tendency, trend, inclination, feeling, or opinion, especially one that is preconceived or unreasoned; PREJUDICE (Word 257)

To Kill a Mockingbird examines the **BIAS** in the South in the 1930s. Lawyer Atticus Finch defends a black man wrongfully accused of a crime just because of the color of his skin. The man's conviction illustrates the deeply-rooted **PREJUDICE** (Word 257) of the times versus judging the charges based on the actual facts.

6 | COMPASSION

NOUN—A feeling of deep sympathy and sorrow for another who is stricken by misfortune, accompanied by a strong desire to alleviate the suffering

In 2015, Pope Francis cleared the way for Mother Teresa to become a saint. Mother Teresa was a beloved nun known for her tireless work with the poor, hungry, and sick in Kolkata, India. She demonstrated her **COMPASSION** for those less-fortunate with her actions and her words. Mother Teresa famously once said:

"*Let us touch the dying, the poor, the lonely and the unwanted according to the graces we have received and let us not be ashamed or slow to do the humble work.***"**

7 | COMPEL

VERB—To drive; to force or submit

Jeffrey Magee earns the nickname "maniac" in *Maniac Magee* because he is **COMPELLED** to run everywhere. His drive to run becomes legendary because no one, including Mars Bars Thompson, can beat Maniac in a foot race. This famous speed develops after his parents' deaths when Maniac must fend for himself and stay on the move.

8 | CONFIDENTIAL

ADJECTIVE—Spoken, written, or acted on in strict privacy or secrecy; secret

---

PRO TIP

Break words into parts: *prefix, root, and/or suffix*

Con + fid + en + tial = confidential
With + trust + in + adj. ending = secrecy

The names of the winners of the Academy Awards are kept **CONFIDENTIAL** by the accounting firm PricewaterhouseCoopers. The information is kept top secret, generating much speculation and suspense in the weeks leading up to Oscar night.

9 | ⭐DEBATE

NOUN—A discussion, an argument, a dispute
VERB—To argue, discuss, deliberate, ponder, or consider

All of the presidential candidates will participate in a **DEBATE** at some point during their election campaign. When candidates **DEBATE**, the audience learns where each of them stands on key issues. Voters will hear each candidate discuss his or her vision for the elected position and what actions they will take if elected. Voters can then make a more informed decision on which candidate to vote for and support.

10 | ⭐DYNAMIC

ADJECTIVE—Pertaining to or characterized by energy or effective action; vigorously active or forceful; energetic

Carli Lloyd is the **DYNAMIC** midfielder who led the U.S. Women's National Soccer Team to victory over Japan in the 2015 World Cup Final. Lloyd's amazing performance included a hat trick; her three goals enabled the American women to win.

11 | ENDORSE

VERB—To approve, support, or sustain

ENDORSEMENT

NOUN—An act of giving one's public approval or support to someone or something; recommendation

Have you ever seen a commercial starring one of your favorite celebrities or athletes? Many companies, like Nike, Coca-Cola, and McDonald's, use celebrity **ENDORSEMENTS** to increase public awareness and create a favorable impression of their products. For example, Peyton Manning **ENDORSES** Papa John's Pizza. Peyton's support of the pizza chain is so strong that he has personally invested in local Papa John's stores in Denver.

12 | FRUGAL

ADJECTIVE—Economical in use or expenditure; prudently saving or sparing; not wasteful

You might think that being a superhero would mean living life like Tony Stark. That's not true for all caped crusaders. Superman, and his alter-ego Clark Kent, is very **FRUGAL**. Unlike Iron Man with his sprawling cliffside mansion and multitude of expensive cars, or Batman with his trusted butler and cave of million-dollar gadgets, Superman, a.k.a Clark Kent, lives in a humble apartment and works as a reporter for *The Daily Planet*.

13 | ★ILLUMINATE

VERB—To supply or brighten with light; to light up; to make lucid or clear

In *Harry Potter and the Prisoner of Azkaban*, Harry uses the Wand-Lighting Charm, Lumos, to **ILLUMINATE** the end of his wand. This light-creation charm casts light in dark places, repels evil spirits, and **ILLUMINATES** the dangers lurking in the shadows.

14 | ★IRONY

NOUN—The use of words to convey a meaning that is the opposite of its literal meaning

> **PRO TIP**
>
> **SITUATIONAL IRONY** is when actions that are supposed to lead to a particular result, in fact, have the opposite outcome.

O. Henry's beloved Christmas story, *The Gift of the Magi*, uses **IRONY** to show a couple's love for each other. The wife decides to sell her hair, which she prizes, in order to afford to buy a watch chain for her husband's pocket watch. **IRONICALLY** (DH Core), at the same time, her husband sells his prized pocket watch in order to afford to buy a jeweled comb for his wife's hair.

15 | JEER

VERB—To ridicule; to taunt; to mock

Red Sox fans are often **JEERED** with insulting remarks when attending a Yankees game. New York fans enjoy ridiculing Boston fans almost as much as they like seeing the Yankees beat the Red Sox.

16 | LUCID

ADJECTIVE—Clear-headed; rational; easily understood; completely intelligible or comprehensible

While most people would have panicked, the young boy remained calm and gave a **LUCID** description of his brother's injuries to the 911 operator. Because the operator had a clear understanding of the situation, he was able to tell the young boy what to do until help arrived.

17 | MORTAL

ADJECTIVE—Subject to dying; human; earthly

Superman is known for his incredible strength and speed. In addition to his ability to fly, Superman also has heightened senses. Despite these powers, Superman is **MORTAL**. If exposed to kryptonite, Superman's powers weaken. If Superman is exposed to kryptonite for too long a period of time, it will kill him. Despite having extraordinary powers, Superman can die just like everyone else.

18 | NAÏVE

ADJECTIVE—Innocent; unsophisticated; inexperienced

In *Inside Out*, Joy is in control of Riley's emotions. Joy fiercely protects Riley's childhood memories, believing that Sadness will ruin Riley's life. Joy is **NAÏVE** to think Riley can live a life without Sadness. In fact, it is the balance that both Joy and Sadness bring to Riley's experiences that enable her to grow and mature.

19 | NOVICE

NOUN—A beginner; someone who is not skilled

Have you ever played *FIFA* with a friend who is totally unfamiliar with the PlayStation controls? It is fun to play a **NOVICE** gamer because it is so easy to beat them. The big wins usually last until the friend figures out the trick to using the controls.

20 | RANCID

ADJECTIVE—Rank, unpleasant, and stale; offensive or nasty; disagreeable

Opening a refrigerator that has been without power for a long time can be an assault on the senses. If the food inside is not kept cold, it will go bad and become **RANCID**. Needless to say, it is necessary to throw out the terrible smelling food.

21 | REMINISCE

VERB—To recall past experiences; to remember

REMINISCENCE

NOUN—The act or process of recalling past experiences or events; a mental impression retained and revived

Successful television programs often have reunion shows many years after the series ends. Viewers enjoy seeing the actors as they are today and hearing them **REMINISCE** about their days on the program. The actors share funny stories and other **REMINISCENCES** about things that happened on the set years ago.

22 | TACIT

ADJECTIVE—Understood without being openly expressed; implied

Sometimes in class it is easy to get distracted and daydream. So, when your teacher makes eye contact with you, it is his or her **TACIT** way of getting your attention.

23 | ★ UNIQUE

ADJECTIVE—Existing as the only one or as the sole example; single; unparalleled; incomparable

Lady Gaga is a talented singer, but she is also famous for her **UNIQUE** fashion choices. Magazine writers cite the raw beef dress she wore for the 2010 MTV Video Music Awards as an example of her one-of-a-kind style.

KNOW YOUR PREFIXES		
LATIN PREFIX:	**UNIFORM**	not changing in form or character; constant
UNI- | one	**UNISEX**	designed for both men and women
	UNICYCLE	a cycle with a single wheel

24 | VARIEGATED

ADJECTIVE—Varied in appearance or color; marked with patches or spots of different colors; varied; diversified; diverse

A favorite **VARIEGATED** treat at Halloween is candy corn. Each piece contains three colors: yellow, orange, and white. There is even a version that has brown on top for chocolate lovers.

25 | WRITHE

VERB—To twist the body about or squirm, as in pain or violent effort

Following even a slight bump, professional soccer players will often fall on the ground, clutching their legs and **WRITHING** in pain. They roll back and forth on the field with agonized expressions on their faces, many times hoping to convince the referees to award a penalty card to their opponent, but other times they are truly hurt.

CHAPTER 1 REVIEW

Match the words to the definitions by writing the definition number next to each word. The answer key is on page 144.

_____ **tacit**	1.	genuine
_____ **unique**	2.	something that is good
_____ **debate**	3.	compassionate
_____ **lucid**	4.	hostile
_____ **writhe**	5.	prejudice
_____ **irony**	6.	to drive
_____ **belligerent**	7.	secret
_____ **jeer**	8.	to argue; an argument
_____ **bias**	9.	energetic
_____ **dynamic**	10.	to approve
_____ **compel**	11.	to supply with light
_____ **variegated**	12.	opposite of literal meaning
_____ **authentic**	13.	to ridicule
_____ **benefit**	14.	clear-headed
_____ **novice**	15.	beginner
_____ **benevolent**	16.	process of recalling the past
_____ **illuminate**	17.	implied
_____ **endorse**	18.	unparalleled
_____ **reminiscence**	19.	varied
_____ **confidential**	20.	to twist in pain

CHAPTER 2

Literary Language

Vocabulary words are important for more than doing well on standardized tests. Chapter 2 contains a list of words from Common Core academic language. These words are vital for classroom discussion and for mastering reading comprehension. In addition to expanding your vocabulary, these words will make you a stronger reader and literary communicator.

26 | ★ANALYZE

VERB—To break down into parts and examine carefully

Readers must **ANALYZE** a passage of text in order to understand its full meaning. This careful examination of all parts of a passage can often reveal subtle **PLOT** (Word 242) points and character insights.

27 | ★ATTITUDE

NOUN—The way a person views something or tends to behave towards it; a belief; a mindset

In the book *Wonder*, Augie Pull, a 10-year-old boy with a facial deformity, is starting at a new school. At the beginning of the year, his classmates' **ATTITUDES** toward him range from acceptance to disgust, but as they get to know him, their perceptions and feelings begin to change.

28 | ★CHARACTERISTIC

NOUN—A trait; a feature

The scar on Harry Potter's forehead is considered a defining **CHARACTERISTIC**. This feature makes it impossible for Harry to mask who he is without using the invisibility cloak or a spell.

29 | ★CONCLUDE

VERB—To bring to a close; to end

★CONCLUSION

NOUN—The end; a summation

When you write a paper, it is very important to always **CONCLUDE** it with a paragraph that wraps up the ideas of the paper. It is essential to restate the main argument in the **CONCLUSION** of your paper. This final paragraph should end the essay and leave the reader something to think about.

30 | ⭐CONNOTE

VERB—To prompt a reader to think about images and ideas beyond a word's literal meaning

When you see Roger Federer play tennis or LeBron James play basketball, it is obvious that both are among the greatest to play their sport. Both Federer and James wear Nike, which is represented by the *Swoosh* logo. The Nike *Swoosh* **CONNOTES** athleticism because so many of the world's top athletes wear the brand.

31 | ⭐CONTEXTUALIZE

VERB—To consider or provide information about the time, place, or circumstances of a story or event

It is common to look back at history and judge it with a modern viewpoint, but it is important to **CONTEXTUALIZE** books like *The Diary of Anne Frank*. The realities of World War II Europe are key to understanding her experiences as a Jew living in the time of World War II and the Holocaust.

32 | ⭐CONTRADICT

VERB—To deny; to present an opposing view

In a courtroom, the job of the defense attorney is to call witnesses who can **CONTRADICT** the evidence presented by the prosecution. The defense uses the opposing testimony to support their view of the evidence and counter the prosecutor's view.

33 | ⭐ CONTRAST

VERB—To show differences between or among
NOUN—Something that is different from something else

In the *The Hunger Games*, life in the Capital **CONTRASTS** with life in District 12. Katniss and her fellow District 12 citizens live poorly with little food and money. On the other hand, people in the Capital have an abundance of food and riches. Their **OPULENT** (Word 179) lifestyle is a **CONTRAST** to the extreme poverty in District 12.

34 | ⭐ DENOTE

VERB—To indicate; to mean something; to show, mark, or be a sign of something

> **PRO TIP**
>
> **CONNOTE** and **DENOTE** sound the same, but they mean different things. **CONNOTE** is when something is implied or hinted, and **DENOTE** is when something is specifically referred to or signified directly.

When scrolling through the pictures on Instagram, we click on the heart to show our friends that we like a picture. The thumbs-up icon on Facebook also **DENOTES** that we like the status update, photo, or link that has been posted by a Facebook friend.

35 | ⭐ FIGURATIVE

ADJECTIVE—A form of language use in which writers and speakers convey something other than the exact meaning of their words; not LITERAL (Word 41)

When you tell your friends that your math test almost killed you, you are using **FIGURATIVE** language. The math test did not **LITERALLY** (Word 41) almost end your life; it was just so hard that it **FIGURATIVELY** felt like it was trying to kill you.

36 | ⭐ILLOGICAL

ADJECTIVE—Contrary or opposed to the fact

Dr. Spock from *Star Trek* only understands data and facts. He finds human emotional reactions **ILLOGICAL**. In one episode of *Star Trek*, Dr. Spock famously stated:

❝*May I say that I have not thoroughly enjoyed serving with Humans? I find their illogic and foolish emotions a constant irritant.*❞

37 | ⭐INDICATE

VERB—To be a sign of; to show

 Sometimes we do not have the time to write a long response to an email or text, so we **INDICATE** our feelings or opinions with emojis and emoticons. It is a quick way to let our friends know what we think or how we feel.

38 | ⭐INFER

*VERB—To form an opinion from evidence; to reach a **CONCLUSION** (Word 29) based on known facts; to hint or suggest*

⭐INFERENCE

*NOUN—A **CONCLUSION** (Word 29) or opinion reached on the basis of evidence and known facts; a presumption*

> **PRO TIP**
> _____
> Context is key! When in doubt, use the sentence or passage to help find or **INFER** the meaning of an unknown word.

A number of questions on reading comprehension tests ask students to **INFER** something from the text. It can be difficult for a student to make an **INFERENCE** because it is not clearly stated in the passage.

Have you ever walked into your class and the teacher asked you to take out a pencil and leave your books on the floor? You can **INFER** from the teacher's instructions and **TONE** (Word 57) of voice that you are about to take a pop-quiz.

39 | ★INTERPRET

VERB—To give or provide meaning of; to explain; to understand a message

Coaches use gestures from the sidelines to call plays. It is the job of the players to **INTERPRET** the signals correctly in order to follow the coach's instructions.

40 | ★INVESTIGATE

VERB—To examine thoroughly, as an idea; to probe; to inquire

In *A Wrinkle in Time,* Meg travels through space and time to **INVESTIGATE** the disappearance of her father. With the help of others, Meg seeks to find out what happened to her dad in order to rescue him.

41 | ★LITERAL

*ADJECTIVE—Completely true; factual; not **FIGURATIVE** (Word 35)*

When blue jeans first arrived in France, there was no **LITERAL** translation for the phrase *blue jeans*. Consequently, *blue jeans* is one of only a few English language words or phrases that have become a part of everyday spoken French.

42 | ⭐OBJECTIVE

*ADJECTIVE—Open-minded; not influenced by personal feelings ;
not **SUBJECTIVE** (Word 52)*

Reporters should be **OBJECTIVE** about the news. They should not include their personal feelings about current events and blur the line between fact and opinion.

43 | ⭐OBSERVE

VERB—To notice or see

⭐OBSERVATION

*NOUN—A statement or point of view based on what has been seen;
an understanding based on first-hand evidence*

OBSERVING photosynthesis is a common science experiment. Students watch plants exposed to different amounts of light and make notes on what they see. These **OBSERVATIONS** illustrate the process and help students better understand the concept.

44 | ⭐PERSPECTIVE

NOUN—Point of view, a way of looking at

Students and teachers can have different **PERSPECTIVES** on grades. Students may feel that a teacher does not like them when they are given a low grade. On the other hand, the low grade is often a way for a teacher to motivate a student to work harder and help them reach the maximum level of their ability.

45 ★ PERSUADE

VERB—To convince; to bring around to one's way of thinking

Benjamin Franklin, John Adams, and Thomas Jefferson were among the most influential leaders of the Continental Congress who **PERSUADED** the other members to declare independence from Britain. Their argument that taxation without representation was unjust was very convincing.

46 ★ PLAUSIBLE

ADJECTIVE—Believable or reasonable, given certain information to consider

> ### PRO TIP
>
> If you add the prefix *im-* to a word, then you negate the meaning of the word because im- means not. **IMPLAUSIBLE** (DH Core) means not **PLAUSIBLE**!

Many feel it is **PLAUSIBLE** that there is life on other planets. These people point to the fact that there is water on Mars, a critical element needed to sustain life.

47 ★ REFLECT

VERB—To think about or consider

Before he signed the Emancipation Proclamation to end slavery, Abraham Lincoln took time to think about his decision and **REFLECT** on the impact it would have on the country. He thought about how freeing the slaves would change the course of the war for the Union and Confederate states. Lincoln also considered how freed black Americans would be permanently transformed.

48 | ⭐RELEVANT

ADJECTIVE—Related to the matter at hand; connected

Students often wonder how **RELEVANT** some of their coursework will be after they graduate. For this reason, many teachers try to incorporate real-life examples into their classes in order to demonstrate the **RELEVANCE** of their course.

49 | ⭐REQUISITE

ADJECTIVE—Needed for a particular purpose

Due to their multiple applications, computers have replaced many of the **REQUISITE** supplies that students needed in the past such as typewriters, slide rules, calculators, and dictionaries. *Direct Hits Vocabulary* is **REQUISITE** to success in school!

50 | ⭐RHETORIC

NOUN—Language that is intended to influence; eloquence

The defense attorney's **RHETORIC** convinced the jury that there was enough reasonable doubt to find the defendant not guilty. The prosecutor felt that the jury was **PERSUADED** (Word 45) by the argument made by the defense attorney rather than the actual facts in the case.

51 | SARCASTIC

*ADJECTIVE—The use of **IRONY** (Word 14) to mock or convey contempt*

Damon Salvatore from *The Vampire Diaries* is often **SARCASTIC**. He once joked about his shortcomings as a vampire:

"*I tried to kill a werewolf; I failed. Now I feel like I'm not living up to the version of my best self.***"**

His snarky attitude can be charming and frustrating because it is hard to tell whether he is being serious or funny.

52 ★ SUBJECTIVE

*ADJECTIVE—Relating to one's own point of view; a matter of taste; opinion; cannot be quantified; not **OBJECTIVE** (Word 42)*

> **PRO TIP**
>
> **OBJECTIVE** and **SUBJECTIVE** are opposites or antonyms.
>
> **OBJECTIVE** = facts
> **SUBJECTIVE** = feelings

Have you ever visited a museum and wondered why a painting is considered a masterpiece? The *Mona Lisa* is widely considered one of the best paintings in the world, but some people think it is an unremarkable portrait of a woman. Each person's point of view shapes the way he or she sees a painting or sculpture. For this reason, many feel that art is totally **SUBJECTIVE**.

KNOW YOUR PREFIXES			
LATIN PREFIX:		**SUBVERT**	to undermine power or authority
SUB-	under; beneath; below	**SUCCINCT** (Word 258)	concise; brief; short
SUC-		**SUMMATION**	a brief or short description of the most important information
SUM-			

53 ★ SUMMARIZE

VERB—To tell information again using fewer words

★ SUMMARY

NOUN—A brief statement that presents the main points in concise form

Movie trailers, like *Star Wars: Episode VII – The Force Awakens*, **SUMMARIZE** the movie with selected scenes from the film. These **SUMMARIES** try to attract an audience by using small clips that hint at the action and plot without giving away too much detail that might spoil the movie.

54 ★ SYMBOLIZE

VERB—To stand for

★ SYMBOL

NOUN—A concrete object that represents an abstract idea

★ SYMBOLIC

ADJECTIVE—Relating to or being used as a symbol; representative

Flowers are used to **SYMBOLIZE** different emotions. Even their colors represent different feelings. A red rose is a **SYMBOL** of love, while a yellow rose stands for friendship, and a white rose is **SYMBOLIC** of purity.

55 | ★SYNTHESIZE

VERB—To combine in order to make something new

Helen Keller became blind and deaf after a childhood illness. In order to communicate, Helen had to **SYNTHESIZE** her sense of touch with her ability to speak to form a new way to interact with people. By combining her working senses, she overcame her handicaps and became an author, an activist, and a public speaker.

56 | ★THEME

NOUN—A unifying idea that is a recurrent element in literary work or artistic work

One **THEME** in *The Lion, the Witch, and the Wardrobe* is the idea of human redemption. Edmund is an unkind boy who manipulates his siblings by helping the White Witch. During the course of the novel, Edmund realizes his mistakes. Ultimately, Edmund's sins are forgiven when Aslan makes a sacrifice to save him. Edmund is changed from an angry, spiteful child into a courageous young man.

57 | ★TONE

NOUN—A quality, feeling, or attitude expressed by the words that someone uses in speaking or writing

From the **TONE** of the coach's remarks, the team could sense how disappointed he was after their opening loss. Resolving to never hear such frustration in his voice again, the players worked hard each week at practice. The **TONE** in the locker room was entirely different at the end of the season after they won the championship.

CHAPTER 2 REVIEW

Use the word bank below to help complete the sentences. NOT all the words are used! The answer key is on page 144.

Word Bank:

analyze	attitude	characteristic
conclusion	connote	contextualize
contradict	contrast	denote
figurative	illogical	infer
indicate	interpret	investigate
objective	observe	perspective
persuade	plausible	reflect
relevant	requisite	resolution
subjective	summary	symbol
synthesize	theme	tone

1. With a competitive _____ like that, your friends will think you will never lose a game!

2. After the tough loss, the team came together to _____ what had gone wrong.

3. Since discovering water on Mars, scientists suspect it is _____ that there is some form of life on the planet.

4. My paper is almost complete; I just need to add a _____ to my essay.

5. The _____ of the book revealed too much of the plot.

6. Describing words are one way to figure out an author's
   _____ .

7. My final grade in the class will be based on an _____
   score that includes my test and quiz grades and a _____
   score that is based on my teacher's opinion of my effort and attitude
   in class.

8. Before we can figure out what really happened, we will
   _____ the scene and question the witnesses.

9. The paragraph about time travel is not _____ to
   the rest of your essay about Thomas Jefferson.

10. I need to compare and _____ World War I and
    World War II for homework tonight.

CHAPTER 3

Words that Count

Vocabulary study isn't just limited to English class! Many words are rooted in math and science, but they have applications beyond these subjects. Words that Count organizes this vocabulary into one chapter with examples that make it easy to understand.

58 | ⭐ ACUTE

ADJECTIVE—Intense; sharp; severe

ADJECTIVE—An angle measuring less than 90 degrees

The **ACUTE** pain the running back felt in his leg indicated that he had broken a bone. The player was devastated because the injury meant that he would not be able to play for the rest of the season.

In geometry, an **ACUTE** angle is one that measures less than 90 degrees.

59 | AMORPHOUS

ADJECTIVE—Without a clearly defined shape or form; vague

PRO TIP

Remember to break down words into different parts!

| **a** | + **morph** | + **ous** | = **amorphous** |
| *without* | + *shape* | + *full of* | = *shapeless* |

My little sister wanted me to describe what shapes I saw in the sky, but the large, **AMORPHOUS** clouds made it difficult to play the game with her.

60 | COLOSSAL

ADJECTIVE—Extraordinarily great in size; gigantic; huge

In its day, the Titanic was the largest passenger steamship ever built, measuring 883 feet. When it set sail on March 31, 1911, from England, everyone believed the boat was unsinkable. Two weeks into its journey to New York, an iceberg sank the **COLOSSAL** cruise liner.

61 | ⭐ CONCAVE

ADJECTIVE—Curved inward like the interior of a circle; hollow and curved in

The **CONCAVE** shape of a satellite TV dish focuses the radio waves received from a transmitting satellite in orbit above the earth onto a small receiver mounted above the dish. The shape focuses the waves creating the TV signal in your home.

62 | ⭐ CONGRUENT

ADJECTIVE—Having identical shapes so that all parts correspond; agreeing; corresponding

The first question on the math test asked the students to draw two **CONGRUENT** triangles. The triangles needed to have identical angles and sides in order to be correct.

63 | ⭐ CONSECUTIVE

ADJECTIVE—Following one another in uninterrupted succession or order; continuous

Netflix has become a very popular way for people to watch television shows. Because a viewer can stream programs, people often watch shows in **CONSECUTIVE** order. It is fairly easy to watch an entire season of a television show over a weekend.

64 | ⭐ CONVEX

ADJECTIVE—Having a surface that is curved or rounded outward

In order to make a chocolate basket, the baker had to flip a mixing bowl over so that it was **CONVEX.** The chocolate sauce was poured over the inverted bowl and hardened. This simple trick formed the perfect chocolate basket.

65 | DEARTH
ADJECTIVE–An inadequate supply; scarcity

The **DEARTH** of rain has caused one the worst **DROUGHTS** (Word 97) in California's history. Residents of the state have been asked to stop watering lawns, washing cars, and even taking baths. The low supply of water is putting a strain on everyone.

66 | DEFICIENT
ADJECTIVE–Insufficient, inadequate

Starbucks's Pumpkin Spice Latte is a popular seasonal drink. However, the company got into trouble with consumers because the drink was **DEFICIENT** in the amount of real pumpkin used. Starbucks changed the ingredients to include an ample amount of real pumpkin.

67 | ★DILATION
NOUN–The widening or stretching of an opening

During any proper eye exam, doctors use dilating drops to expand the pupils in order to check the interior of the eyes. The **DILATION** from the drops lasts from 4 to 24 hours. For this reason, patients are not allowed to drive a car until their pupils have returned to normal size.

68 | ⭐EQUIVALENT

ADJECTIVE—Equal in value, measure, force, effect, significance

It is important to know about equal values. For example, four quarters are **EQUIVALENT** to one dollar bill, and three feet are equal to one yard.

KNOW YOUR PREFIXES		
LATIN PREFIX:	**EQUITABLE**	fair and impartial; even-handed
EQUI- | equal	**EQUIDISTANT**	at equal distances
	EQUILATERAL	having all sides of the same length

69 | ⭐ESTIMATE

VERB—To form an approximate judgment or opinion of something; to evaluate

Fantasy football sites **ESTIMATE** a player's upcoming points performance based on the player's history against the opponent and the number of points earned in the past few weeks. Fantasy matchups are won and lost based on individual players meeting or exceeding their projected points.

70 | FINITE

*ADJECTIVE—Having bounds or limits; restricted; not **INFINITE** (Word 72)*

In order to maintain order and safety, music festivals like Lollapalooza can only sell a **FINITE** number of tickets. The limited number helps the festival draw a lot of people without creating chaos.

71 | IMMENSE
ADJECTIVE—Vast; huge; very great

Due to the **IMMENSE** popularity of the FIFA video games and the World Cup tournament, Americans are becoming increasingly fascinated with professional soccer. Teams like Arsenal and Manchester United now have large fan bases in America.

72 | INFINITE
*ADJECTIVE—Immeasurably great; endless; not **FINITE** (Word 70)*

Scientific **OBSERVATIONS** (Word 43) and data show that the universe is endlessly expanding. Some scientists suggest that the **INFINITE** nature of our universe leads to possibilities of life on other planets.

73 | NULL
ADJECTIVE—Without value

Confederate money was introduced in April, 1861, at the start of the Civil War. The purpose of the money was to separate the Confederate States of America's economy from the Union's economy. When the South lost the Civil War, Confederate currency was declared **NULL** and void. Consequently, large numbers of southerners lost all of their wealth and fell into poverty.

74 | NUMEROUS
ADJECTIVE—Very many; being or consisting in great quantity

The **NUMEROUS** opinions and motivations of the original thirteen colonies created a conflict in the days leading up to the

Revolutionary War. The concerns of some of the colonies differed greatly from the worries of others. It took over a year from the time the first shots were fired in Massachusetts for the Declaration of Independence to be adopted by the Second Continental Congress.

75 | ★OBTUSE

ADJECTIVE—Not quick or alert in perception; dull
ADJECTIVE—An angle that measures greater than 90 degrees

Walt Disney Studios Motion Pictures uses the slow-witted arche-type in many of their movies. Examples of these **OBTUSE** characters include Dopey from *Snow White and the Seven Dwarfs*, Horace and Jasper from *101 Dalmatians*, Scuttle from *The Little Mermaid*, Le Fou from *Beauty and the Beast*, Rex from *Toy Story*, and Olaf from *Frozen*. Although their simpleminded antics provide comic relief, they often make up for their intellectual limitations through their loyalty and kindness.

In geometry, an **OBTUSE** triangle has one angle that measures more than 90 degrees.

76 | ★OUTLIER

NOUN—Something or someone that lies outside the main body or group; an outcast

The Catcher in the Rye is one of the classic novels about an **OUTLIER.** Holden Caulfield is a teenager who feels that he is an outcast. As the narrator of the novel, Holden describes his struggles trying to fit in with the world around him.

77 | ⭐ PERIMETER

NOUN—The border or outer boundary

Many homeowners secure the **PERIMETER** of their homes with alarm systems and motion detecting lights. The security around the outside of the house acts as a deterrent to anyone who might think about breaking into the home.

78 | PERPETUAL

ADJECTIVE—Continuing or enduring forever; everlasting

New York City is nicknamed "The City that Never Sleeps." For those who live there or visit, the **PERPETUAL** street noise of car horns and delivery trucks proves the nickname true.

79 | POLYMORPHOUS

ADJECTIVE—Having, taking, or passing through many different forms or stages

> **PRO TIP**
>
> The prefixes Poly- and A- are antonyms.
>
> Poly = many, A= without

Amphibians, such as frogs, are **POLYMORPHOUS** creatures. They start as egg masses that grow into tadpoles. The tadpoles develop legs and slowly leave the water for land. The tadpoles then transform into young frogs with tails. Once the tails fall off, the frogs become adults.

80 | ★ PROOF

NOUN—The evidence sufficient to establish something as true; demonstration

Experiments are the way that scientists find the **PROOF** needed to support a hypothesis. As an example, by gathering evidence scientists have been able to demonstrate that the universe is expanding.

81 | REMOTE

ADJECTIVE—Far apart; distant

The Sentinelese people live on a distant island off the coast of eastern India. This **REMOTE** tribe has lived on their island for an estimated 60,000 years. The Sentinelese avoid all contact with the outside world, choosing to live far apart from modern society in complete isolation.

82 | SCANT

ADJECTIVE—Barely sufficient; inadequate

The Sumatran Tiger is considered critically endangered. **ESTIMATED** (Word 69) to be fewer than 400, the **SCANT** number of Sumatran Tigers roaming wild in Indonesia has many wildlife experts concerned that the species will become extinct by 2020.

83 | ★SYMMETRY

NOUN—Similarity, correspondence, or a balance of systems or parts of a system

Did you know that snowflakes follow mathematical rules? The **SYMMETRY** of the snowflake is illustrated by the identical patterns on each of the snowflake's arms.

KNOW YOUR PREFIXES

LATIN PREFIX:	SYMPHONY	harmony of sounds
SYM- | same	SYMPATHY	harmony of feelings
	SYMBIOSIS	a mutually beneficial relationship between people or groups

84 | ★VARIABLE

ADJECTIVE—Likely to change; fluctuating

San Francisco is a relatively small city, measuring seven square miles. Despite its size, it has some of the most **VARIABLE** weather zones of any city in the U.S. On any given day, it can be cold and foggy on the ocean side of the city while it is warm and sunny by the bay. For this reason, anyone living in San Francisco knows to always dress in layers before they leave the house.

CHAPTER 3 REVIEW

Write the word from the Word Bank next to the correct definition. The answer key is on page 144.

Word Bank:

amorphous   congruent   consecutive   dearth

equivalent   finite   immense   outlier

remote   variable

1. _____ Far apart; distant

2. _____ Having identical shapes so that all parts correspond

3. _____ Equal

4. _____ Following one another in uninterrupted succession or order; continuous

5. _____ Something or someone that lies outside the main body or group; outcast

6. _____ Likely to change; fluctuating

7. _____ Vast

8. _____ Without a clearly defined shape or form

9. _____ Having bounds or limits

10. _____ An inadequate supply

CHAPTER 4

Planet Earth

There is a whole world of language that comes from our planet. Chapter 4 has collected these commonly used all-natural words so you can easily learn them and apply them to class-work and essay writing.

85 | ABYSS

NOUN—A deep immeasurable space; a deep chasm

Due to the high pressure and frigid temperatures, humans have been unable to survey the deep canyons and gorges of the ocean floor, making it one of the final frontiers of exploration. In recent years, scientists have developed a vehicle that is able to investigate the **ABYSS**. Finally, the deep, hidden valleys of the ocean can be studied.

86 | ⭐ AGRICULTURE

NOUN—The science or occupation of cultivating land; farming

AGRICULTURE is essential for the survival of modern society. California produces more food than any other state in the U.S. Milk, cheese, artichokes, garlic, olives, strawberries, and grapes are just a few examples of the food that comes from California. It is incredible to think that so much of the nation's food is sourced from one state.

87 | ALBINO

NOUN—An animal or plant with a marked deficiency of pigmentation

The only known white humpback whale lives off the coast of Australia. The **ALBINO** is easy to spot in the water because his appearance is so different than the other whales in his pod.

88 | ARID

ADJECTIVE—Being without moisture; extremely dry; parched

The Atacama Desert in northern Chile receives only 0.6 inches of rainfall a year, making it the driest place on earth. In fact, it is so

ARID that there are some places where it is **ESTIMATED** (Word 69) that there has been no rainfall in over 400 years. Remarkably, the region received nearly seven times its average annual rainfall in the spring of 2015, causing long-buried seeds to sprout and flowers to bloom.

89 | AZURE

ADJECTIVE—Clear blue; serene

Hawaii is a tropical paradise. The islands are famous for their lush rainforests and **AZURE** water. Scuba divers and snorkelers are able to view a variety of sea life in the clear, calm, vibrant blue Hawaiian waters.

90 | BOUGH

NOUN—A large branch of a tree

Building a treehouse requires more than a detailed set of instructions. The foundation of any treehouse is a suitable tree with a strong trunk and sturdy **BOUGHS** to provide much-needed support. With the right tree and a creative plan, a treehouse makes for a fun building project!

91 | ⭐BOUNDARY

NOUN—Something that indicates limits; border

A fence is a common **BOUNDARY** between yards. It marks the border of an individual's property. As the saying goes, good fences make for good neighbors!

92 | ★CONSTELLATION

NOUN—A group of stars that is known by a recognized name
NOUN—A group or cluster of related things

Orion is one of the easiest **CONSTELLATIONS** to find in the sky. Orion is most clearly visible in January, and it is usually located by finding the three stars on his belt.

93 | CONTAMINATE

VERB—To make impure or unsuitable by contact or mixture with something unclean or bad; to pollute

The BP oil spill in 2010 created many concerns for people living on the Gulf Coast. One serious worry was that the chemicals in the oil had **CONTAMINATED** the plant life and sea life. This had a negative impact on the fishing industry because people were afraid to eat any seafood caught in the Gulf of Mexico.

94 | CULTIVATE

VERB—To grow and care for something; to foster

Organic farming is a trend that is spreading across the country. It can be challenging to produce a healthy, organic harvest. Farmers must **CULTIVATE** the planting area before any organic seeds are planted. First, the soil is fertilized with all-natural matter like compost. Plants are fortified with non-chemical pest control and organic plant food. Finally, farmers rotate crops so that the planting area is not overused, which helps with natural soil development. It takes years of hard work to create a **ROBUST** (Word 132) organic farm.

95 | DILUTE

VERB—To make thinner or weaker by the addition of water or a similar substance

> ### PRO TIP
> ---
> Draw pictures or cartoons for hard to remember vocabulary words.

People are particular about their coffee. Many people love a strong, black cup of coffee in the morning. Others, however, **DILUTE** their coffee with milk. The addition of milk weakens the coffee so it is not as strong tasting. Some people also add sugar to lessen the natural bitterness of coffee. The perfect cup of coffee is totally **SUBJECTIVE** (Word 52)!

96 | DOMESTIC

ADJECTIVE—Of or relating to the home or homeland; native

Some voters are concerned about problems in our home country while others focus more on conflicts and natural disasters abroad. Politicians must balance **DOMESTIC** issues, such as healthcare and education, with global needs like foreign aid and international terrorism.

97 | DROUGHT

NOUN—A period of dry weather; an extended shortage

Severe **DROUGHT** can destroy crops and hurt the food supply. In recent years, the continent of Africa has struggled with extended periods of dry weather, which has led to many millions of people facing starvation.

98 | ERODE

VERB—To eat into or away; to deteriorate

The Grand Canyon is one of the natural wonders of the world. For millions of years, the Colorado River has **ERODED** the rock on the riverbed. The **PERPETUAL** (Word 78) flow of water wears at the rocks, forming the deep river valley between the Grand Canyon's plateaus.

99 | EXCAVATE

VERB—To remove by digging; dig out

King Richard III of England was killed in battle in 1485. His burial site was a mystery until 2012 when his remains were discovered in Leicester, England. Archaeologists **EXCAVATED** the skeleton from under the former site of an ancient church. Once his identity was confirmed through DNA testing, King Richard III was reburied at Leicester Cathedral.

100 | ★EXPLORE

VERB—To examine; to investigate; to probe

Lewis and Clark led an expedition to the west coast. The adventurers **EXPLORED** the new territories of the Louisiana Purchase westward. The goal of the expedition was to map a route from the Mississippi River to the Pacific Ocean.

101 | FISSURE

NOUN—A long, narrow crack

Scientists have discovered that glaciers contain **NUMEROUS** (Word 74) **FISSURES** filled with seawater. Despite the presence of these cracks, most of the glaciers are not breaking apart. Scientists believe that these crevices act like sponges, allowing the glacier to absorb and release water as needed.

102 | FLOURISH

VERB—To be in a vigorous state; to thrive

If a garden is planted with care, plants of all varieties will **FLOURISH**. All it takes is good soil, sunlight, water, and fertilizer to **CULTIVATE** (Word 94) a garden that produces different flowers, fruits, and vegetables.

103 | HYBRID

ADJECTIVE—Formed from two different elements or varieties

HYBRID engines have become very popular in recent years. The combination of electric and gas motors is the most common. One **BENEFIT** (Word 2) of driving a car with a **HYBRID** engine is better fuel efficiency, so the owner will save money on gas.

104 | ★INHABIT

VERB—To live or dwell in a place; to reside

Coyotes, usually thought of as rural animals, now **INHABIT** urban areas. Coyotes have been spotted in New York City. Wildlife experts believe that they are arriving via the bridges into the city and are adapting to the noise and chaos of city living.

105 | LUMINOUS

ADJECTIVE—Emitting or reflecting steady, suffused, or glowing light; beaming

Sirius, also known as the Dog Star, is the most **LUMINOUS** star in the Earth's night sky. It is so bright that the name actually means 'glowing' in Greek. Ancient Egyptians based their calendar on when Sirius became visible in the eastern sky.

106 | PRECIPICE

NOUN—The steep face of a cliff

Wingsuit flying is an extreme sport growing in popularity. Jumpers propel themselves off a **PRECIPICE** with their arms extended like wings. The specially designed suit the jumper wears enables him or her to experience wind-propelled flight like a bird.

107 | TERRAIN

NOUN—The natural physical features of a tract of land

An all-**TERRAIN** vehicle is able to drive across almost any type of land. It is particularly good for crossing low-lying bodies of water and maneuvering steep, rocky areas.

KNOW YOUR ROOTS		
LATIN PREFIX:	TERRITORY	any tract of land
TERR- earth	**SUBTERRANEAN**	underground
TERRA-	**EXTRATERRESTRIAL**	outside the limits of the earth

108 | TOIL

VERB—To work under difficult and physically challenging conditions; to labor

Miners in coal country **TOIL** underground or inside the rock face removing coal from the earth. It is very difficult work with limited light and fresh air. Adding to the danger of their work is the threat of a cave-in or damage to their lungs from long-term exposure to coal dust.

109 | VISAGE

NOUN—Face

George Washington has the most recognizable **VISAGE** in the United States. His face is at the center of the dollar bill. As our first President, his image is in **NUMEROUS** (Word 74) portraits, paintings, and books. His **VISAGE** is even chiseled on Mt. Rushmore along with three other Presidents.

110 | WANE

VERB—To decrease in strength and intensity

The moon goes through different phases approximately every 28 days. At midpoint of the cycle, the moon is completely **ILLUMINATED** (Word 13) and is a full moon. Over the next 14 days, the visible glow **WANES**. The moon seems to decrease in size until it is barely visible.

111 | ZENITH

NOUN—The highest point, peak

Mount Everest is the tallest mountain in the world, measuring 29,029 feet at its **ZENITH**. Reaching the summit is very challenging. Many climbers attempt it every year, but very few succeed due to the thin air, extreme cold, and unpredictable weather.

CHAPTER 4 REVIEW

Match the words to the definitions by writing the definition number next to each word. The answer key is on page 145.

_____ **abyss**	1.	to examine; to investigate
_____ **cultivate**	2.	farming
_____ **zenith**	3.	to thrive
_____ **arid**	4.	clear blue; serene
_____ **contaminate**	5.	an extended shortage
_____ **wane**	6.	to dig out
_____ **excavate**	7.	to deteriorate
_____ **agriculture**	8.	the steep face of a cliff
_____ **domestic**	9.	pollute
_____ **fissure**	10.	deep chasm
_____ **azure**	11.	to decrease in strength and intensity
_____ **flourish**	12.	reside
_____ **inhabit**	13.	face
_____ **drought**	14.	extremely dry
_____ **explore**	15.	a group of related things
_____ **precipice**	16.	a long, narrow crack
_____ **dilute**	17.	weaken
_____ **visage**	18.	to grow
_____ **erode**	19.	the highest point
_____ **constellation**	20.	native

CHAPTER 5

All About Adjectives

Have you ever had a teacher ask you to be more descriptive or add some variety to your vocabulary in an essay? If so, this chapter is for you! Adjectives are awesome, and they are words that easily improve your writing. Direct Hits has collected a whole chapter of some of our favorite adjectives. Use a few of these in your next writing assignment, and you will be amazed by how happy your teacher will be!

112 | ADEPT

ADJECTIVE—Very skilled at something; expert

David Price was a star pitcher for Vanderbilt University from 2005 until he graduated in 2009. After Vanderbilt, the Tampa Bay Rays drafted Price. His **ADEPT** pitching earned him the starting position at the 2010 All-Star Game. On December 4, 2015, Price's expert skills were rewarded with a seven-year, $217 million contract with the Boston Red Sox.

113 | AGILE

ADJECTIVE—Able to move quickly and easily; deft

Handball and table tennis are very popular in Asia. It is likely that you may have only seen these sports played competitively during the Olympics, but did you know that these two sports require athletes to be tremendously **AGILE**? Believe it or not, handball and table tennis require more quickness and coordination than boxing, gymnastics, or basketball!

114 | AMIABLE

ADJECTIVE—Friendly and pleasant; generally agreeable

PRO TIP

Remember that adjectives describe nouns! Adjectives are words that relate to our 5 senses: *sight, smell, taste, touch, and hearing.*

Stargirl is a very friendly person as a new student at Mica High School. Stargirl becomes famous among her peers for her **AMIABLE** nature by playing her ukulele and singing *Happy Birthday* in the cafeteria to anyone celebrating a birthday.

115 | APATHETIC

ADJECTIVE—Lacking interest or concern; indifferent

As soon as an NFL team is eliminated from the playoffs, that team's fans often feel **APATHETIC** toward the playoff season. Interest often returns for the Super Bowl because, more than just a game, it is entertaining television due to the special commercials and over-the-top halftime show.

116 | ASTUTE

ADJECTIVE—Mentally sharp or clever; smart

The **ASTUTE** student noticed that the teacher had mistakenly marked one of her answers incorrect on the test. After class, she spoke to the teacher about the mistake she had caught and received three points back on her test grade.

117 | BRASH

ADJECTIVE—Confident and aggressive; bold

Miley Cyrus is considered a **BRASH** celebrity in the media. Her confident and outspoken nature is criticized because it is so different from her former wholesome, girl-next-door *Hannah Montana* persona.

118 | COMPETENT

ADJECTIVE—Having the necessary ability or skills

Airline pilots undergo intense testing and training before obtaining their certification to fly a passenger plane. In addition, pilots take ongoing training and tests to ensure that they continue to be **COMPETENT** to fly. The responsibility of flying large numbers of people from one place to another demands up-to-date knowledge as well as quick and accurate reactions to any problems.

KNOW YOUR PREFIXES		
LATIN PREFIX:	**COMPETE**	take part in a contest
COM- together;	**COMBINE**	merge or bring together
CON- with	**COMPOSE**	to come together to make something
	CONCEIVE	form a plan
	CONCOCT	prepare or cook by mixing ingredients together
	CONFER	to discuss something with someone else

119 | CONGENIAL

ADJECTIVE—Having the same nature, disposition, or tastes; agreeable

Many tourists consider Central Park the most **CONGENIAL** part of New York City. Visitors enjoy the park because of its open spaces and hidden gardens. Central Park has the reputation for being the most agreeable spot for families in Manhattan.

120 | CONVENTIONAL

ADJECTIVE—Based on what is generally done or accepted; customary

In a fast food restaurant, it is **CONVENTIONAL** to pay for your meal when you order it. In a restaurant with waiters, it is typical to pay for your meal after you have finished eating and are ready to depart.

121 | CORPULENT
ADJECTIVE–Large or bulky; fat

America's second President, John Adams, was an intelligent and accomplished man long before reaching the office of the President. His **CORPULENT** physique and small stature made it easy for people to mock him. His friends and detractors nicknamed President Adams "His Rotundity" as a way to mock his weight.

122 | DEVOUT
ADJECTIVE–Deeply religious

Thousands of **DEVOUT** Catholics traveled long distances in order to see Pope Francis in New York and Philadelphia when he visited in 2015. Even though most of them only saw him as he drove by on his way to an event, seeing the Pope was a once-in-a-lifetime experience for these deeply religious Catholics.

123 | DUBIOUS
ADJECTIVE–Unsure or uncertain, feeling doubt about something

Many scientists are **DUBIOUS** about reported alien sightings. There is limited scientific evidence that the alien encounters occurred. Often the sightings are found to be pranks carried out by individuals with a good camera and some knowledge of special effects.

124 | EMACIATED

ADJECTIVE—Abnormally thin

The rescue group was shocked by the condition of the abandoned horse. It was **EMACIATED** and lacked any energy. After receiving water and food, the horse slowly started to gain weight and look better.

125 | EXUBERANT

ADJECTIVE—Very happy, lively, or energetic; vivacious

Kevin Hart is an **EXUBERANT** comic. His lively and energetic stand-up routine is focused on life as a short man. He happily mocks himself in front of audiences.

126 | IMMACULATE

ADJECTIVE—Perfectly clean; pristine

Sheldon Cooper likes to keep his living space and office **IMMACULATE**. His character on *The Big Bang Theory* is obsessed with a neat and perfectly clean environment. If anything is out of order or dirty, Sheldon becomes very stressed.

127 | INDIGNANT

ADJECTIVE—Feeling or showing anger because of something that is unfair or wrong

Teenagers become **INDIGNANT** when parents want to monitor their social media activities. Many feel it is an unfair invasion of privacy, but parents believe it is important to be informed about what is being posted and what their children are being exposed to online.

128 | INTREPID

ADJECTIVE—Very bold or brave; fearless

Solo free climbing is a sport that has grown in popularity over the years. Climbers can only use their hands, feet, and body as support to scale rock walls. **INTREPID** individuals choose to pursue this dangerous activity because it is the ultimate risk-taking sport. A successful free climb means that the person has faced a circumstance that could likely kill him and overcame it.

129 | JUBILANT

ADJECTIVE—Feeling or expressing great joy; very happy

Traveling the world as global music stars has its **BENEFITS** (Word 2), but even rock stars get homesick. The band *5 Seconds of Summer* was **JUBILANT** about being back in Australia after being away for such a long period of time. Each member was overjoyed to be home and play a concert for adoring fans.

130 | MALICIOUS

ADJECTIVE—Having or showing a desire to cause harm to someone; mean

The Governor became a **MALICIOUS** dictator in *The Walking Dead*. He started as a well-intentioned leader, but circumstances led the Governor to become cruel and inhumane. He tortured and killed people without regret or guilt.

KNOW YOUR PREFIXES		
LATIN PREFIX:	**MALIGNANT**	evil in nature; deadly
MAL- | bad; wrong	**MALICE**	intention to cause harm; ill will
	MALADY	a disease or illness

131 | PUNY

ADJECTIVE—Of less than normal size and strength; weak

Ants are some of the smallest insects on the planet. However, these seemingly **PUNY** creatures are actually capable of carrying 5,000 times their body weight.

132 | ROBUST

ADJECTIVE—Strong; healthy

Some people wake up with the sun ready to start the day. Other people struggle to get going in the morning and need a **ROBUST** cup of coffee to get them energized for the day.

133 | TIMID

ADJECTIVE—Demonstrating a lack of confidence; shy

It is not always easy for students to participate in class. **TIMID** people prefer to stay quiet and go unnoticed. Unfortunately, some teachers mistake shyness for a lack of interest or knowledge; however, the silent student in the back of the room is often the one thinking the most about the discussion.

134 | VERSATILE

ADJECTIVE—Able to adapt to many different situations or activities; flexible

Hugh Jackman is known as one of Hollywood's most **VERSATILE** actors. Although Jackman is most famous as the superhero

Wolverine, you may also have seen him star in many serious roles on film. Additionally, he has won two Tony awards for his work on Broadway. Not only can Hugh Jackman out-brute enemies, but he can sing and dance too!

135 | VIGILANT
ADJECTIVE—Keeping a careful watch

A lifeguard at the pool or on the beach must be **VIGILANT** at all times. Whether scanning the deep pool for an inexperienced child struggling to swim or the horizon for a surfer in trouble, a lifeguard must be ready to leap into action at a moment's notice.

136 | ZEALOUS
ADJECTIVE—Having or showing enthusiasm

Olaf is the **ZEALOUS** snowman in *Frozen*. He loves summer more than just about anything else. Unfortunately, his enthusiasm for hot and sunny days is **IRONIC** (DH Core) since he is made of snow.

CHAPTER 5 REVIEW

Use the word bank below. The answer key is on page 145.

Word Bank:

agile	amiable	competent	dubious
malicious	robust	timid	zealous

Word: _____

Definition in your own words:

_____

Word: _____

Definition in your own words:

_____

Word: _____

Draw it:

Word: _____

Draw it:

Word: _____

Use the word in a sentence that helps explain what it means.

_____

_____

Word: _____

Use the word in a sentence that helps explain what it means.

_____

_____

Word: _____

Use the word in a sentence that helps explain what it means.

_____

_____

Word: _____

Use the word in a sentence that helps explain what it means.

_____

_____

CHAPTER 6

This Day in History

History is more than just names and dates; it is also a wonderful world of words. Each word in this chapter is contextually used with historical examples. Not only will this chapter improve your vocabulary, it will also help with history class!

137 | ABDICATE

VERB—To renounce or relinquish a throne, right, power, claim, or responsibility, especially in a formal manner

In 1936, Edward VII, King of England, decided to **ABDICATE** the British throne. He relinquished his crown, choosing his love for a divorced American woman over his royal duties, which caused quite a scandal at the time.

138 | AFFILIATION

NOUN—The state of being associated

The American Revolution was a challenging time in our country's history. Patriots supported America's independence from Great Britain while Loyalists continued to back the crown. Loyalists were a minority during the Revolution, and their **AFFILIATION** with and support of King George III and the British army often put them at odds with members of their own family fighting on the side of American independence.

139 | ANIMOSITY

NOUN—A feeling of strong dislike

In December 1921, Ireland was divided into two parts. The Republic of Ireland became independent from the United Kingdom while Northern Ireland remained part of the union. Unfortunately, **ANIMOSITY** between Catholics and Protestants in Northern Ireland fueled violent clashes between the two Christian denominations, which sadly resulted in the deaths of thousands of Northern Irish.

140 | ⭐AUTHORITY

NOUN—The power or right to control, judge, or prohibit the actions of others

Historically, the reigning King or Queen in Great Britain had absolute **AUTHORITY** over England, Scotland, Wales, and colonies and territories around the world. In modern day Great Britain, the Queen's power is mostly **SYMBOLIC** (Word 54) because the British Parliament and Prime Minister are responsible for introducing new laws and changing old ones.

141 | BRANDISH

VERB—To shake or wave something; to display

Samurai warriors were the mighty fighters in ancient Japan. Their dominance in battle was known around the world. The Samurai were especially famous for their sword-fighting skills. When an enemy saw a Samurai **BRANDISH** his sword, the Samurai's **NEMESIS** (Word 228) must have feared for his life!

142 | ⭐CONTENTIOUS

ADJECTIVE—Tending to strife; argumentative

Slavery and states' rights were two of the causes for the Civil War. Abolitionists grew increasingly **CONTENTIOUS** about the practice of slavery in the South. By 1830, the Abolitionist Movement had grown in political power and influence. Southern states argued that the federal government had no **AUTHORITY** (Word 140) to regulate or abolish slavery in individual states. This strife between the North and the South created a divide that ultimately led to the secession of the Southern states.

143 | DECREE

NOUN—A formal or authoritative order

On October 3, 1863, President Abraham Lincoln issued the Thanksgiving Proclamation. This **DECREE** established the last Thursday in November as a national day of giving thanks. Thanksgiving is traditionally celebrated with a big turkey meal on the fourth Thursday in November every year.

144 | DISCORD

NOUN—Conflict between people or nations; disagreement

Prior to the Revolutionary War, disagreement began to develop between the colonies and the crown over taxes. Specifically, colonists were unhappy with new taxes imposed by King George III. Essentially, the king wanted the colonies to pay for the debt he incurred during the French and Indian War. Anger increased as the colonists felt that they were being taxed without a fair voice in British Parliament. The slogan 'No taxation without representation' expressed the **DISCORD** between the colonies and the crown.

KNOW YOUR PREFIXES		
LATIN PREFIX:	**DISALLOW**	to refuse to allow; reject
DIS- | not	**DISCONNECT**	to break the connection with something; cut off
	DISRESPECT	a lack of respect; rudeness

145 | ENDEAVOR

NOUN—A strenuous effort, an attempt
VERB—To exert oneself; to strive

The goal of the 1804 Lewis and Clark Expedition was to find a transcontinental passageway to the Pacific Ocean. Meriwether Lewis and William Clark **ENDEAVORED** to map a safe westward route to the northwest coast. Their **ENDEAVOR** was filled with many life-threatening moments. They were fortunate to meet Native Americans during their travels who helped them navigate their way from St. Louis to Fort Clatsop, Oregon.

146 | ERADICATE

VERB—To destroy completely; to obliterate

Diseases like polio and yellow fever have not been a threat to Americans for decades, but they persist in other countries. The only disease stamped out across the globe is smallpox. In 1980, the World Health Organization stated that smallpox had been **ERADICATED** worldwide. It is very challenging to eliminate a disease all over the world, which is why there has only been one in recorded history.

147 | FOREBEAR

NOUN—An ancestor

Finding Your Roots is a popular television series on PBS. Celebrity guests research their family history as far back as records allow. While many of the stories are interesting and heartwarming, some stories of the **FOREBEARS** are upsetting. Whether it is discovering that a great-great-grandmother was sold in the slave trade or that an ancestor sailed over on the Mayflower, these historical accounts document a family's heritage.

KNOW YOUR PREFIXES		
LATIN PREFIX:	**FORECAST**	predict in advance
FORE- | before	**FORESHADOW**	to indicate in advance
	FOREWORD	an introductory statement to a book

148 | HYSTERIA

NOUN—An uncontrollable outburst of emotion or fear

The Salem Witch Trials of 1692 were the result of a great deal of fear about witchcraft in colonial Massachusetts. The **HYSTERIA** spread throughout the colony as people feared that young women were possessed by the devil. Nineteen people were hanged after being convicted of witchcraft while 150 more men, women, and children were accused. Sadly, the deaths and accusations were all based on unexplained illnesses that fueled an irrational panic.

149 | INGENUITY

ADJECTIVE—The quality of being clever

The Wright Brothers are credited with the first manned motor-powered flight. After much research and reading on the subject, Wilbur Wright believed that he could design a powered flying machine. On December 17, 1903, the first successful flight took place in Kitty Hawk, North Carolina. It lasted only 12 seconds. After more research and development of the design, the Wright Brothers' **INGENUITY** paid off, and the brothers founded the Wright Company, which built the first U.S. military plane.

150 | LOCOMOTION

NOUN–The power to move to one place or another

The introduction of the railroad transformed westward expansion in America. Prior to the 1800s, **LOCOMOTION** was limited to horses and wagon trains. Initially, short lines were built to move raw materials to factories and manufactured goods to markets, but the completion of the transcontinental railroad on May 10, 1869, permanently revolutionized commerce and transportation in the U.S.

151 | MANDATE

VERB–To order; to command
NOUN–An authoritative order or command

During the Vietnam War, the U.S. government **MANDATED** that men join the armed forces. This **MANDATE** stated that men had to register for the military and receive a draft number when they turned eighteen. If their number was called, they were forced to sign up and serve.

152 | PILFER

VERB–To steal; thieve

The largest theft in history happened at the Central Bank of Iraq on March 18, 2003. The day before coalition forces began their attacks, Saddam Hussein's son **PILFERED** the bank, stealing one billion U. S. dollars. Ultimately, about $650 million was recovered, but $350 million of the money has never been found.

153 | PLIGHT
NOUN—An unfortunate condition or state

Life on the Great Plains was not easy for people, but the **PLIGHT** of the farmers became far more difficult in the 1930s. **DROUGHT** (Word 97) destroyed the crops, and high winds created large dust clouds that swept across the dry land. The territory impacted by this devastating era in American **AGRICULTURE** (Word 86) became known as the Dust Bowl. Not only did the harsh conditions kill crops, they choked livestock to death. Ultimately, 60% of the population was driven from parts of Kansas, Colorado, Oklahoma, Texas and New Mexico.

154 | PRAGMATIC
ADJECTIVE—Dealing with things sensibly; practical

Grover Cleveland is considered the most **PRAGMATIC** president in U.S. history. He is remembered as being hardworking, honest, and bland. Unlike presidents before him, Cleveland was not interested in making thousands of political appointments for his party or proposing legislation that was favorable to friends. Rather, he believed in a small, efficient government and felt that the role of president was to be a watchdog over Congress rather than actively engage in legislation. Cleveland is the only president elected to two non-consecutive terms.

155 | PRUDENT

ADJECTIVE—Showing care and thought for the future; wise

When World War I broke out in Europe, the U.S. did not think it was **PRUDENT** to choose a side. At the time, World War I was viewed as a dispute between European countries rather than a global issue. The policy of the U.S. at the start of the war was to remain neutral, believing that very little would be gained if the U.S. entered the conflict. Feelings changed when the Germans started torpedoing U.S. supply ships in the Atlantic. Very quickly, the government and everyday Americans realized that the wiser choice was to join the Allies against Germany.

156 | QUARANTINE

NOUN—A state of isolation

VERB—To impose a condition of isolation

After the bombing of Pearl Harbor, the U.S. government stated that people of Japanese ancestry needed to live in isolated camps so that they would not pose a threat to national security. On February 19, 1942, President Roosevelt ordered the deport-ation or incarceration of anyone of Japanese ancestry. Those who remained in the U.S. were **QUARANTINED** in internment camps. Japanese-Americans were in **QUARANTINE** in central parts of California as well as Idaho, Utah, Arizona, Wyoming, Colorado, and Arkansas.

157 | ★ RATIFY

VERB—To approve

In December of 2015, 187 countries came to a concensus on a climate change agreement. While the proposals were settled upon in Paris, each country now must **RATIFY** the accord. Leaders and climate change advocates are hopeful that all participating countries will approve the Paris Climate Change Agreement within the next couple of years.

158 | RAZE

VERB—To completely destroy; to demolish

During the Vietnam War, the U.S. military used napalm as a weapon of war. Bombs loaded with napalm **RAZED** entire villages and sections of jungle. Chemicals and gasoline created huge firestorms that obliterated anything in their path. While napalm was considered an effective military weapon for many years, it has come to **SYMBOLIZE** (Word 54) the cruelty and devastation of war.

159 | RELINQUISH

VERB—To voluntarily give up; to renounce

The 37th President of the United States, Richard Nixon, resigned on August 9, 1974. Nixon had to **RELINQUISH** the office because of his involvement in the Watergate scandal. Nixon's administration was involved in illegal activities, including breaking into the Democratic Party headquarters at the Watergate complex. Nixon is the only president to ever have resigned from office.

160   REVERE

VERB—To feel deep respect for something

REVERENCE

NOUN—A deep respect for someone or something

Arlington National Cemetery is one of the most **REVERED** places in America. It is the final resting place for more than 400,000 citizens who have died in service to the U.S., including soldiers from the Civil War. There are ceremonies throughout the year that demonstrate the nation's **REVERENCE** for this honored place. The job of any serviceperson is appreciated, but none are more respected than those who sacrificed their lives.

161   SEVER

VERB—To divide by cutting or slicing; to separate

On January 3, 1961, the U.S. **SEVERED** diplomatic ties with Cuba. President Eisenhower closed the U.S. embassy in Havana, which cut relations with Fidel Castro and his communist regime. Over the course of many decades, the U.S. and Cuba have improved their relationship enough that the U.S. reopened its embassy in Havana on August 14, 2015.

162   TURMOIL

NOUN—A state of great confusion and uncertainty; upheaval

As Rome grew from a small city-state to a vast empire, **TURMOIL** arose. It was challenging for the Roman government to maintain control over territories that spanned thousands of miles. The inability to govern effectively from a great distance created increasing poverty and corruption that ultimately led to the collapse of the empire in 476 C.E.

163 | ZEAL

NOUN—A strong feeling of interest that makes someone very eager to do something; enthusiasm

ZEALOT

NOUN—A person who has very strong feelings about something; an extremist

> **PRO TIP**
>
> If you come across a word you don't really know, think of a similar word and use the meaning. For example, the word **ZEAL** (Word 163) can be found in **ZEALOUS** (Word 136).
>
> *Zeal = great enthusiasm for something.*

During her short life, many considered Joan of Arc a religious **ZEALOT**. Joan, disguised as a man, joined the French army to fight the British in the Hundred Years War. Joan claimed that God sent her messages in visions about saving France from its enemies. The **ZEAL** Joan exhibited about her belief that God was speaking directly to her caused many at the time to question whether she was involved with witchcraft. The English famously burned her at the stake for being a witch. Twenty years after her death, she was found innocent of all charges. In 1920, Joan of Arc was canonized as a saint by the Catholic church.

CHAPTER 6 REVIEW

Write the word next to the correct definition. The answer key is on page 145.

Word Bank:

animosity	authority	discord	eradicate
hysteria	ingenuity	mandate	prudent
ratify	turmoil		

1. _____ The power or right to control, judge, or prohibit the actions of others

2. _____ To destroy completely

3. _____ The quality of being clever

4. _____ To order; to command
An authoritative order or command

5. _____ To approve

6. _____ Conflict between nations or people

7. _____ A feeling of strong dislike

8. _____ A state of great confusion

9. _____ Showing care and thought for the future

10. _____ An uncontrollable outburst of emotion or fear

CHAPTER 7

Celebrity Sightings

It's not just celebrities making headlines! These famous words are often found alongside pictures of your favorite stars. Next time you are gossiping about Kanye or Taylor, use these words to sound like an expert!

164 | ADMONISH

VERB—To warn or caution against something; to scold

Many celebrities get frustrated with the attention paid to them by the paparazzi, and some have creatively **ADMONISHED** the photographers. On a morning stroll in New York City, Emma Stone and Andrew Garfield covered their faces with cards that gave information on charities to support. Garfield's card read:

"*www.youthmentoring.org, www.autismspeaks.org, (and don't forget) www.wwo.org, www.gildasclubnyc.org. Here's to the stuff that matters. Have a great day!***"**

It was an effort to scold the paparazzi for focusing on fame instead of more important issues.

165 | ALLEGE

VERB—To claim or assert without proof; to accuse

A couple of years ago, Justin Bieber's neighbor **ALLEGED** that the singer had thrown at least a dozen eggs at his house, causing over $20,000 in damage. The singer initially denied the claim that he was the **PERPETRATOR** (Word 206) of the egging. Ultimately, the Biebs pled no contest to the vandalism and was ordered to pay over $80,000 in compensation.

166 | APPREHENSIVE

ADJECTIVE—Uneasy or fearful that something bad might happen; anxious

J.J. Abrams is one of Hollywood's busiest writers and directors. Before achieving success on shows like *Lost* and with movies like *Super 8* and *Star Trek*, he was a massive *Star Wars* fanboy.

Needless to say, J.J. was extremely **APPREHENSIVE** when he was asked to write and direct *Star Wars: Episode VII – The Force Awakens*. Mr. Abrams's biggest worry was that he would disappoint moviegoers because fans of the original trilogy might not accept his vision of the final chapters of the story.

167 | CHIDE

VERB—To scold

Stage actors need the respect and silence of the audience in order to immerse themselves in the action on the stage. Audience members are expected to turn their phones off during performances out of respect for everyone in the theater; however, every now and again an audience member forgets to silence their phone. Kevin Spacey **CHIDED** an audience member at his one-man show in London for failing to quiet his phone. After hearing a few rings, Spacey, in character, scolded:

"*If you don't answer that, I will!***"**

The audience applauded the unscripted line.

168 | CLICHÉ

NOUN—Anything that has become commonplace because of overuse; stereotype

Romantic comedies are a genre of movies that rely heavily on commonplace situations for two characters to meet and fall in love. Popular **CLICHÉS** in romantic comedies include the couple meeting in a bookstore and kissing in the rain. Even dystopic romantic couples like Katniss and Peeta find time to steal a smooch in the rain!

169 | DEROGATORY

ADJECTIVE—Showing a disrespectful attitude; insulting

At the start of the 2016 Presidential primary campaigns, many candidates tried to focus their speeches and participation in the candidates' debates on their personal, positive qualifications to be President and the policies they planned to implement, if elected. As the campaigns progressed, candidates found that making **DEROGATORY** comments about other candidates, whether true or not, improved their standing in the polls more than their own qualifications.

170 | ECSTATIC

ADJECTIVE—Full of joyful excitement; elated

When LeBron James announced he was returning to the Cavaliers after several seasons with the Miami Heat, Cleveland fans were **ECSTATIC** to welcome the Ohio-born James home. Fans gathered at the arena to celebrate the homecoming of "King James".

171 | GARRULOUS

ADJECTIVE—Very talkative; excessively chatty

The host of *The Tonight Show*, Jimmy Fallon, has a reputation for being **GARRULOUS** during his interviews. Because he is so friendly and outgoing with his celebrity guests, Jimmy can be a bit too chatty, leaving little time for the guests to discuss the projects they have appeared on the show to promote.

KNOW YOUR SUFFIXES		
LATIN SUFFIX:	**JOYOUS** (DH Core)	full of joy
-OUS | possessing; full of a quality	**NERVOUS**	full of anxiety; tense
	DANGEROUS	full of danger

172 | GAUDY

ADJECTIVE—Distastefully flashy; tacky

Lots of celebrities drive fancy cars like Porsches and Ferraris. Nicki Minaj is no exception as she bought a $400,000 Lamborghini in 2013. Because it was not showy enough for Nicki, she custom-painted her Lamborghini bright pink. The **GAUDY** car made it easy to spot Nicki on the streets of L.A.!

173 | GLUTTONY

NOUN—Habitual greed; excess

The Kardashian family embodies celebrity excess. Between their homes, cars, and accessories, their **GLUTTONY** is their brand. They market themselves in the media as the ultimate consumers and make millions of dollars every year by tweeting about products or being photographed wearing a certain accessory. For example, a photograph that Kim Kardashian tweeted of herself wearing a waist-trimming corset caused sales of the corset to skyrocket.

174 | IMITATION

NOUN—A thing or person intended to copy something or someone; an impersonation; a caricature

IMITATE

VERB—To mimic or impersonate; to copy

Tina Fey is one of the most well-known comics in Hollywood. One of her most memorable moments came while still part of the cast on *Saturday Night Live* when she **IMITATED** Sarah Palin in a sketch. Her impersonation was so perfect that people found it difficult to tell the real Sarah Palin apart from Tina Fey's character. The **IMITATION** was so popular that Sarah Palin participated in a skit on *SNL* playing herself alongside Tina's impersonation of her.

175 | INFAMOUS

*ADJECTIVE—Well known for a bad reputation; **NOTORIOUS** (Word 178)*

> **PRO TIP**
> _____
> Suffixes can help you determine parts of speech.
> -OUS words are ALWAYS adjectives!

O.J. Simpson was once famous for his football skills and post-football broadcasting and acting career. That all changed when his wife and a friend were murdered. O.J.'s **INFAMOUS** white Bronco police chase down an L.A. freeway and subsequent trial for double homicide are what come to mind when most people hear the name O.J. Simpson. All of his prior accomplishments have been overshadowed by his downward spiral.

176 | LAPEL

NOUN—One of the two folds of fabric below the collar on each side of a coat or jacket

Celebrities support various charitable causes. One way they bring attention to a cause is to wear **LAPEL** pins to public events. Perhaps the most recognizable **LAPEL** pin is the pink ribbon signifying support for breast cancer research. Politicians also wear American flag **LAPEL** pins to show patriotism.

177 | LAVISH

ADJECTIVE—Luxurious; fancy

George Clooney and his wife, Amal, hosted a **LAVISH** wedding weekend in Venice, Italy. Celebrity friends like Matt Damon were treated to fancy parties, gourmet food, and a wedding ceremony at the luxurious hotel Aman Canal Grande Venice, which was originally a 16th century Venetian palace.

178 | NOTORIOUS

ADJECTIVE—Famous for a bad reputation; INFAMOUS (Word 175)

Justin Bieber is **NOTORIOUS** for his wild antics and poor behavior, such as egging his neighbor's house (see Word 165 **ALLEGE**) or illegally racing exotic cars at high speeds. He is now attempting to change his bad reputation by focusing media attention on his music rather than his shocking conduct. Only time will tell if Bieber is sincere in his attempts to clean up his act.

179 | OPULENT

ADJECTIVE—Very expensive; luxurious; grand

A large and expensive home is a status symbol for many celebrities. Drake recently purchased a $7.7 million compound in Hidden Hills, California. The **OPULENT** home features a movie theater, spa and massage room, pool, tennis court, and mechanical bull. With such **LAVISH** (Word 177) amenities, it is hard to imagine Drake wanting to leave home!

180 | OSTENTATIOUS

ADJECTIVE—Characterized by an obvious show to impress others; ***GAUDY*** *(Word 172)*

> **PRO TIP**
>
> Suffixes = part of speech!
> - **-ous**   = adjective
> - **-ed**   = past tense verbs
> - **-ion, -cion** = noun
> - **-sion, -tion**

Mariah Carey became engaged to Australian billionaire James Packer in January 2016. Mariah Carey's **OSTENTATIOUS** diamond engagement ring is 35 carats or the size of a large grape! The ring is reported to have cost somewhere between $10 million and $16 million. With that size ring, Mr. Packer is showing the world how rich he is!

181 | RANT

NOUN—A spell of ranting; a tirade
VERB—To speak or shout in a wild way

Twitter **RANTS** are a popular mode of expression for celebrities. Kanye's tirades on Twitter are almost as famous as the man himself. His epic tweets are rambling, amusing, and confusing. Lately, Kanye has **RANTED** about in-app purchases and the violence in Disney movies.

182 | RAVE

NOUN—An enthusiastic review of something; praise
VERB—To talk wildly
ADJECTIVE—Enthusiastic

Star Wars: Episode VII – The Force Awakens was one of the most eagerly anticipated films of 2015. The social media **RAVES** about the film's trailer suggested that the movie would be a huge success, but the studio and producers were uncertain whether fans of the franchise and movie critics would **RAVE** about *The Force Awakens* once it was released to theaters. To everyone's relief, the movie received mostly **RAVE** reviews as some people thought it was as good as the original.

183 | RENDEZVOUS

NOUN—A meeting at an agreed time and place; an appointment
VERB—To meet at an agreed time and place

Did you know many celebrities notify the paparazzi before heading out of the house? Publicists will give photographers the location of their clients, and the photographers **RENDEZVOUS** with the stars casually exiting Starbucks or the gym looking like they just stepped out of the pages of a magazine. The planned **RENDEZVOUS** is positive publicity for the celebrities and money in the pockets of the lucky paparazzi snapping the pictures.

184 | SHREWD

ADJECTIVE–Having smart powers of judgment; intelligent

Taylor Swift is renowned for her songwriting and singing; however, she is also a **SHREWD** businesswoman. Taylor uses social media like Instagram and Twitter to interact with her fans. Additionally, she has controlled her image by trademarking certain phrases, such as "This Swift Beat," and buying "Taylor Swift" domain names so that her image cannot be used in a negative way. These **ASTUTE** (Word 116) business decisions, along with her music success, have made Taylor a very wealthy woman.

185 | TEDIOUS

ADJECTIVE–Long and tiresome, boring; dull

Did you ever want to know a model's favorite sandwich or the Starbucks drink that a particular actress likes to enjoy after her yoga class? If you follow a celebrity on Twitter or Instagram, these **TEDIOUS** details become common knowledge.

186 | VERBOSE

ADJECTIVE–Using more words than are needed; wordy;
***GARRULOUS** (Word 171)*

It is fun to watch award shows to see the clothes, accessories, and dates of movie and music stars. The anticipation of the envelope opening and winner announcement is another reason that people tune in to the Oscars or the Grammys. Less enjoyable are the **VERBOSE** acceptance speeches that some of the winners feel they need to give. At times the winner is so wordy that the music starts to play and the microphone is cut off!

CHAPTER 7 REVIEW

Use the word bank below. The answer key is on page 145.

Word Bank:

chide	ecstatic	gluttony	lapel
notorious	opulent	rant	shrewd

Word: _____

Definition in your own words:

_____

Word: _____

Definition in your own words:

_____

Word: _____

Draw it:

Word: _____

Draw it:

Word: _____

Use the word in a sentence that helps explain what it means.

_____

_____

Word: _____

Use the word in a sentence that helps explain what it means.

_____

_____

Word: _____

Use the word in a sentence that helps explain what it means.

_____

_____

Word: _____

Use the word in a sentence that helps explain what it means.

_____

_____

CHAPTER 8

So The Story Goes

Reading comprehension can be a challenge for many students. Whether it is discussing a novel in class or answering reading comprehension problems, understanding vocabulary in a story is key to school success. These more advanced words are incorporated into examples from books read for school and for fun.

187 | ADORN

VERB—To add beauty; to decorate

In *Catching Fire*, President Snow is determined to launch the latest Quarter Quell promoting the marriage of Peeta and Katniss. He **MANDATES** (Word 151) that Katniss wear her wedding dress for her television interview with Cinna. Katniss arrives at the interview in her wedding dress that is **ADORNED** in silk and pearls. She describes the dress as:

"Heavy white silk with a low neckline and tight waist and sleeves that fall from my wrists to the floor. And pearls. Pearls everywhere. Stitched into the dress and in ropes at my throat and forming the crown for the veil."

188 | AKIN

ADJECTIVE—Of similar character; related

The Outsiders is a coming-of-age story about a gang of poor kids in Oklahoma who are in conflict with the rich gang from the west side of town. Ponyboy Curtis's narration is **AKIN** to a memoir as he reflects on the motivations and dynamics of the family, friends, and foes that **INHABIT** (Word 104) his world.

189 | BUNGALOW

NOUN—A small cottage

Jane Austen's *Sense and Sensibility* follows the lives of the Dashwood women. They face financial hardship after the death of Mr. Henry Dashwood because his fortune and the family home are given to his son, John, by his first wife. John moves himself and his family into the home immediately after the funeral and sends his stepmother and half-sisters to fend for themselves. This change in circumstance leads the women to move into a **BUNGALOW** on a friend's estate. The cottage is small and cozy with a beautiful garden. While the Dashwood women come to love their new space, they all miss the family home terribly.

190 | CLING

VERB—To hold tight

The True Confessions of Charlotte Doyle is a historical fiction adventure story about a young girl sailing to America from England to join her family. Charlotte's time on the ship is full of risk and danger. At one point during her journey, the ship sails into the middle of a hurricane. Despite the violence of the storm, the captain orders Charlotte to climb one of the masts to cut down a sail. Charlotte **CLINGS** to the ropes in an effort to avoid being tossed out to sea by the wind and rain.

191 | COMATOSE

ADJECTIVE—In a state of unconsciousness

Some fairytales are a little scary by nature. For example, *Sleeping Beauty* is the story of an envious witch and a young girl. Maleficent appears before newborn Aurora and curses her to die on her 16th birthday. The quick-thinking fairies alter the spell so it will put the princess to sleep rather than kill her. The girl lies **COMATOSE** until the kiss of her true love awakens her. Even though it ends happily, *Sleeping Beauty* is a dark tale of jealously.

192 | DAWDLE

VERB—To waste time; to linger

Hamlet is one of Shakespeare's most famous characters. The play by the same name centers on the death of Hamlet's father. A son seeking revenge for his father's death **CONNOTES** (Word 30) a story full of adventure. On the contrary, Hamlet **DAWDLES** over what to do. He is certain that his mother and uncle are involved, but he spends most of the time thinking about what to do rather than doing anything. It is not until the last act of the play that Hamlet stops wasting time and finally takes action!

193 | DILAPIDATED

ADJECTIVE—In a state of disrepair or ruin

Prior to running away from home, Huck Finn is locked up in a **DILAPIDATED** cabin by his abusive father. Huck fears for his life, so he fakes his own death in order to escape the cabin. He hides on an island in the middle of the Mississippi River while everyone searches for his body in the water. *The Adventures of Huckleberry Finn* starts out as a depressing story of a mistreated boy, but it quickly grows into a tale of great adventure and hope.

194 | DURATION

NOUN—The length of time something lasts

Across Five Aprils is the story of the Creighton family at the time of the Civil War. The novel opens at the start of the war as Jethro Creighton remains at home while his brothers and cousins head off to battle. For the **DURATION** of the novel, Jethro struggles with the fallout of the war and its impact on his family.

195 | FALLIBLE

ADJECTIVE—Capable of making mistakes; not accurate

PRO TIP

Suffixes can help you determine parts of speech.

-IBLE words are ALWAYS adjectives!

Holden Caulfield is not only one of literature's most memorable narrators; he is also one of its most **FALLIBLE**. *The Catcher in the Rye* is told from his point of view, so the reader has to determine what to believe and what not to believe. In the novel, Holden admits his tendency to stretch the truth:

"*I'm the most terrific liar you ever saw in your life. It's awful. If I'm on my way to the store to buy a magazine, even, and somebody asks me where I'm going, I'm liable to say I'm going to the opera. It's terrible.***"**

KNOW YOUR ROOTS

LATIN SUFFIX:		AGREEABLE	pleasant; appealing
-ABLE	capable of being	EDIBLE	fit to be eaten
-IBLE		FORGETTABLE	easily forgotten

196 | HAUGHTY

ADJECTIVE—Arrogantly superior; conceited

The **HAUGHTY** Caroline Bingley, sister of Charles Bingley in *Pride and Prejudice*, believes that she and her family are superior to the Bennet sisters. Caroline manipulates her brother in an attempt to stop him from falling in love with Jane Bennet. She is also terrible to Elizabeth because she is jealous of the attention Elizabeth receives from Mr. Darcy.

197 | HINDER

VERB—To create difficulties for something or someone; to thwart

Frodo is tasked to deliver the ring of power to Modor in *The Lord of the Rings* trilogy. His journey is dangerous as many around him want the ring. One character, in particular, **HINDERS** Frodo every chance he can. Gollum desires the ring more than anything, so he tries to befriend Frodo and help him complete his task. In actuality, Gollum leads Frodo into circumstances that obstruct Frodo's success and open up opportunities for Gollum to steal the ring.

198 | HOVEL

NOUN—A small, very humble house

Prior to heading to the Quarter Quell in the *The Hunger Games*, Katniss Everdeen and her family live in poverty in District 12. The family's **HOVEL** is dirty and without heat. Katniss does the best she can to keep the house in decent shape for her mother and sister. She even hunts outside the fence in order to provide food.

199 | INSOLENT

ADJECTIVE—Showing an arrogant lack of respect; rude

In *Charlie and the Chocolate Factory*, Veruca Salt gets her Golden Ticket after demanding that her rich father force his workers to unwrap as many chocolate bars as it takes to find a ticket. She is completely spoiled, and Willy Wonka does not appreciate her **INSOLENT** behavior. After demanding that Mr. Wonka hand over one of his trained squirrels, she is labeled a "bad nut" and is sent out of the factory by the garbage chute. Veruca Salt ends up rejected and covered in trash!

200 | IRATE

ADJECTIVE–Characterized by great anger; furious

Christmas is a time of holiday lights and festive music, but that time of year always made the Grinch **IRATE**. He hated the lights and the tree; the singing of holiday songs made him mean. For a long time, the residents of Whoville avoided the Grinch and his angry ways.

201 | LAMENT

VERB–To express deep sorrow; to grieve

Augustus Waters does not want Hazel grieving his death in *The Fault in Our Stars*. He hosts a pre-funeral funeral so he can see what will be said about him after he is gone. Hazel reads what she thinks will be her eulogy for Gus. She **LAMENTS** Gus's illness and impending death, and the pre-funeral funeral also allows Gus to infuse some humor and laughter into a very sad situation.

202 | LENIENT

ADJECTIVE–Permissive; not strict

Harry Potter is required to live under the stairs at his aunt and uncle's house while his cousin, Dudley, gets whatever he wants. Harry's aunt and uncle are very strict with him, forcing him to do chores and sending him to spend hours hidden away under the stairs. On the other hand, the Dursleys are very **LENIENT** with Dudley despite the fact that he is a spoiled brat who is very mean to Harry. Dudley is rarely, if ever, punished for his bad behavior.

203 | MEANDER

VERB—To wander aimlessly

Into the Wild documents the last years of the life of Christopher McCandless. After graduating from Emory University, Christopher heads west in his car. In an attempt to isolate himself from civilization, Christopher spends the next 18 months or so **MEANDERING** across the western half of the U.S., making his way to Alaska. Sadly for the McCandless family, his need to wander in the great outdoors led to his untimely death.

204 | OMEN

NOUN—An occurrence seen as sign of future happiness or disaster

The tragic ending in *Romeo and Juliet* is foreshadowed throughout the course of the play. At the end of the night after first meeting Juliet, Romeo comments:

"… *my mind misgives some consequence yet hanging in the stars shall bitterly begin his fearful date with this night's revels and expire the term of a despised life, closed in my breast, by some vile forfeit of untimely death.***"**

Romeo receives another **OMEN** when he dreams that he is dead and Juliet's kiss brings him back to life. Unfortunately for Romeo, his dream is a prediction of what is to come.

205 | PATHETIC

ADJECTIVE—Evoking pity; wretched

Gary Paulsen's memoir, *My Life in Dog Years*, is a **REFLECTION** (Word 47) of his life based on the relationships with his dogs. Quincy, a tiny mutt that Paulsen rescues, is one of the best stories in the book. Paulsen finds a very **PATHETIC** Quincy seeking shelter at a woman's home in Alaska.

"*When I first saw Quincy he looked like a dust mop that had been dropped in grease and rolled in old coffee grounds.***"**

Paulsen takes Quincy back home with him, and the fierce, tiny dog ends up being the fearless protector of Paulsen's wife. At one point Quincy saves Paulsen's wife from a bear! The transformation from a pitiful, homeless mutt to beloved guardian is pretty amazing.

206 | PERPETRATOR

NOUN—A person who commits a crime

The tension in *Roll of Thunder, Hear My Cry* reaches its **ZENITH** (Word 111) when a lynch mob comes looking for T.J. A fire breaks out in the cotton field, which forces the black farmer and lynch mob to work together to stop the fire from spreading; it also saves T.J.'s life. At the time of the fire, everyone assumes that a lightning strike caused the field to go up in flames. As it turns out, Papa is the **PERPETRATOR**; he started the fire to save T.J. from the lynch mob.

207 | PRECOCIOUS

ADJECTIVE—Having advanced mental development at an early age; mature

The central character in *Extremely Loud & Incredibly Close* is a **PRECOCIOUS** 9-year-old boy, Oskar Schell. After his father dies, Oskar sets out on a mission to discover the meaning of a key that his dad left behind. This young boy struggles with issues that are very mature. At the end of the novel, Oskar intelligently reflects on what he has discovered:

"*I don't believe in God, but I believe that things are extremely complicated, and her looking over me was as complicated as anything ever could be. But it was also incredibly simple. In my only life, she was my mom, and I was her son.***"**

208 | PROCURE

VERB—To obtain something

Summer of My German Soldier tells the story of 12-year-old Patty Bergen and the German soldier, Anton, whom she hides after he escapes a prison camp. While hiding him, Patty must **PROCURE** food and clothing for Anton. By helping Anton, Patty puts her family and herself in a potentially dangerous situation with the F.B.I. Even though Patty is Jewish, she struggles with the fact that her family and her town see the Nazi soldiers as evil when she knows Anton to be a good person who never wanted to be part of Hitler's army.

209 | PROPHESY

NOUN—A prediction

In *Harry Potter and the Sorcerer's Stone*, the **PROPHESY** of Harry's role in the demise of Voldemort is the reason he is hidden away with his uncle's family. The prediction puts Harry's life at risk since Voldemort wants to kill him before Harry can fulfill his destiny.

210 | RUE

VERB—To bitterly regret

Homer's *The Odyssey* is the epic poem about the incredibly long journey of Odysseus. The poem details the temptations and obstacles that Odysseus faces trying to return home to his wife and son. At one point, Odysseus encounters a fierce storm at sea that might kill him. Rather than regretting that he may never see his wife, child, and home again, Odysseus **RUES** that he may lose his life at sea rather than gloriously die in battle. His chief concern is that he wants his death to be celebrated for its bravery rather than be forgotten and lost at sea. Odysseus's love of fame exceeds his love of home and family.

211 | SLOVENLY

ADJECTIVE—Messy and dirty

All Quiet on the Western Front examines World War I from the perspective of a young German soldier, Paul Baümer. Paul is sent to the trenches in the French battlefront. Life in the horrible and **SLOVENLY** trenches is nothing like what Paul expected it to be. It is filthy and messy and littered with injured and dead men.

"*Trenches, hospitals, the common grave—there are no other possibilities.***"**

Paul watches as the reality of this harsh existence changes his friends and him forever.

212 | SURLY

ADJECTIVE—Ill-tempered and unfriendly; sullen

Ebenezer Scrooge is the **INFAMOUS** (Word 175) main character in *A Christmas Carol*. The **SURLY** old man has no kind words for anyone, especially his employee, Bob Cratchit. On Christmas Eve, Scrooge is visited by by three ghosts who hope to show him how his unkind and angry nature isolates him from the goodness and happiness of the world around him.

213 | VILLAIN

NOUN—A character whose evil actions are central to the PLOT (Word 242)

After a plane crash leaves a group of choirboys stranded on an island, Jack emerges as the **VILLAIN** in *Lord of the Flies*. Without the rules and boundaries of the civilized world, Jack's **INNATE** (DH Advanced) evil appears. He leads a small group in rebellion against the elected leader, Ralph. He murders a fellow stranded choirboy. His brutality and violence are all the more terrifying because he is only 12 years old.

214 | VINDICTIVE

ADJECTIVE—Inclined to revenge; vengeful

Buck from *The Call of the Wild* is a once-tame dog that finds his wild instincts through a series of unfortunate circumstances. Buck's life and death struggles **REFLECT** (Word 47) the survival efforts of his human companions. When Buck's best friend, a man named Thornton, dies, Buck changes into a **VINDICTIVE** character seeking to avenge his friend's death. By the end of the story, none of Buck's gentleness remains, and he embraces his wild nature and becomes the leader of a pack of wolves.

CHAPTER 8 REVIEW

Use the word bank below to help complete the sentences. NOT all the words are used! The answer key is on page 146.

Word Bank:

adorn	duration	lament	procure
akin	fallible	lenient	prophesy
bungalow	haughty	meandered	rue
cling	hinder	omen	slovenly
comatose	hovel	pathetic	surly
dawdle	insolent	perpetrator	villain
dilapidated	irate	precocious	vindictive

1. The _____ child recited the Preamble to the Constitution at her birthday party.

2. The charming _____ was located close to a duck pond and a strawberry patch.

3. We _____ along the shoreline looking for seashells.

4. We could not believe the _____ attitude of the salesperson; she treated us as though we had no money to spend in her boutique!

5. We became _____ after sitting on the tarmac for seven hours without food or water.

6. The police finally caught the _____ of the bank robbery.

7. _____ parenting can sometimes lead to ill-mannered children.

8. I thought the three black crows outside my window might be an _____ for a bad day.

9. The _____ old man shouted at the kids to stay off his lawn and not play on the street in front of his house.

10. The injured driver was _____ in the intensive care unit; the doctors could not say whether or not his condition would improve.

11. Some people _____ their Christmas trees with lots of decorations and lights while others like to keep it simple with clear lights and only a few ornaments.

12. Everyone has an opinion on their favorite _____; it is difficult to choose between Voldemort and Loki.

CHAPTER 9

Taskmasters, Tasks, and Tools

Everybody has to make a living! This chapter is dedicated to jobs and tools and the people using them. If you want to achieve your academic goals, employ these words and put them to work for you.

215 | BENEFACTOR

NOUN—Someone who helps another person or group by giving money; a patron

Charities rely on the generosity of **BENEFACTORS**. Without their donation of large amounts of money, organizations like the Red Cross would not be able to carry out their missions of helping people in need.

216 | CHOREOGRAPHER

NOUN—A person who creates dance sequences, especially for stage and screen performances

Paula Abdul may be best known as one of the original *American Idol* judges, but she is also a respected **CHOREOGRAPHER**. Paula has worked with many artists over the years creating dance sequences for music videos and concert tours.

KNOW YOUR SUFFIXES		
LATIN SUFFIX:	**AUTOGRAPH**	a signature
GRAPH- | write	**BIOGRAPHY**	a written account of someone else's life
	PHOTOGRAPH	a picture made using a camera

217 | CLEAVER

NOUN—A tool with a heavy, broad blade

CLEAVERS are essential tools for butchers around the world. Although they vary in size, most **CLEAVERS** resemble a rectangular hatchet. The powerful, sharp blade makes it easy for butchers to chop through bones and slice thick meat.

218 | COLLABORATOR

NOUN–A person who works jointly with other people

COLLABORATE

VERB–To work jointly with others; to cooperate

Pharrell Williams **COLLABORATES** with many musicians. When he worked jointly with Daft Punk on the song *Get Lucky*, it became Daft Punk's first number-one single on the charts. Pharrell was also a **COLLABORATOR** on the song *Blurred Lines*, writing and producing the song while Robin Thicke provided the vocals.

219 | COMMENTATOR

NOUN–A person who discusses important people or events

Unlike the quiet golf announcers, most sports **COMMENTATORS** are loud and enthusiastic with plenty of opinions to share. For example, NFL **COMMENTATORS** offer pregame predictions, halftime evaluations and recommendations, and postgame summaries, as well as play-by-play analysis throughout the game. There is no shortage of commentary for any football matchup!

220 | ⭐COMMUNITY

NOUN–A unified body of individuals; a neighborhood

The Walking Dead **EXPLORES** (Word 100) the challenges of building a **COMMUNITY** after the zombie apocalypse. Strangers must come together in order to protect themselves from the zombies and other humans fighting for survival.

221 | COUNSEL

NOUN—Advice given to someone
VERB—To give advice to someone

The doctor **COUNSELED** his patient that the best course of treatment was a mix of medicine and acupuncture. The patient valued the doctor's **COUNSEL**, but chose to get a second opinion.

222 | ENTOURAGE

NOUN—One's attendants or associates

Kim Kardashian and Kanye West travel with a large **ENTOURAGE**. They have nannies for their children, stylists, bodyguards, and publicists who fly with them all over the world. These associates are vital in maintaining the Kim and Kanye brand.

223 | FELON

NOUN—One who has committed a serious crime; a criminal

In many states, convicted **FELONS** lose their right to vote. Local governments state that committing a serious crime against an individual is the same as committing a crime against society, so these criminals are not allowed to participate in any election.

224 | GOURMAND

NOUN—Someone who enjoys good food, often to excess

Food blogs and food review sites are commonplace these days. It seems that everyone has an opinion about the food they eat. Whether dining at fancy restaurants or local food trucks, **GOURMANDS** publish their food editorials, encouraging others to indulge in mouthwatering meals and delicious desserts!

225 | INCISION

NOUN—A surgical cut made into skin or flesh

When surgeons perform operations on their patients, their hands must be steady and strong to make precise **INCISIONS**. While a scalpel is the main tool used, some surgeons operate using lasers to make very small cuts. The smaller the **INCISION**, the smaller the scar will be, and the faster the cut will heal.

226 | INDICTMENT

NOUN—A formal charge or accusation of a crime

Before a district attorney moves forward with a case, the **ALLEGED** (Word 165) criminal is served with an **INDICTMENT**. The **INDICTMENT** lists the crimes the person is accused of having committed.

227 | PROPOSE

VERB—To put forward an idea or plan; to suggest

The job of Congress is to detemine, debate, and suggest new laws. Congress **PROPOSES** new bills at each session. Before a bill can be sent to the President to sign into law, it must pass committee discussion, a House of Representatives vote, and a vote by the Senate.

228 | NEMESIS

NOUN—A rival or opponent that is difficult to defeat; an enemy

Ultron is considered the greatest **NEMESIS** of the Avengers. Ultron is the enemy robot of all mankind, and he embodies the fear humans have of a technology becoming evil. Ultron threatens the Avengers and humanity, declaring:

"Do you see the beauty of it? The inevitability? You rise, only to fall. You, Avengers, you are my meteor. My swift and terrible sword and the Earth will crack with the weight of your failure. Purge me from your computers; turn my own flesh against me. It means nothing! When the dust settles, the only thing living in this world... will be metal!**"**

229 | OPPOSITION

NOUN—A competitor or adversary; a disagreement expressed through actions or words

★ OPPOSE

VERB—To disagree with or disapprove of; to defy

The Democrats and Republicans **OPPOSE** each other's viewpoint so much that it has become very hard to pass legislation in Congress. Regardless of which party is in power, both sides regularly disagree with the **OPPOSITION**'s legislative ideas. This extreme level of **DISCORD** (Word 144) has frustrated a majority of Americans.

230 | SKEPTIC

NOUN—A person inclined to question or doubt something accepted as factual; a doubter

SKEPTICAL

ADJECTIVE—Relating to or having the characteristic of a doubter; disbelieving

MythBusters stars two **SKEPTICAL** hosts, Adam Savage and Jamie Hyneman. The premise of the show is to be a **SKEPTIC** and doubt everything. Each episode challenges common myths using scientific experiments.

231 | SURROGATE

NOUN—A substitute

Every now and again, a teacher will take a sick day or a personal day. When this happens, a substitute teacher leads the class. Sometimes the teacher's **SURROGATE** faces a **DUBIOUS** (Word 123) classroom of students. It is not always easy to manage a group of kids who would rather talk or Snapchat than complete the assignment from the absent teacher!

232 | TYRANT

NOUN—Someone who uses power in a cruel and unfair way

Hitler is one of history's most infamous **TYRANTS.** After he was elected, Hitler threw out the German constitution and ruled through force. Hitler was also instrumental in the breakout of World War II, which resulted in the deaths of millions of people.

233 | VEND

VERB—To sell something

> **PRO TIP**
>
> Use your knowledge of foreign language to help with unknown words!
>
> Spanish: vender = sell
> French: vendre = sell

For many years, street vendors have sold souvenirs and simple food items like pretzels and hot dogs to people looking for a bargain or needing a quick bite of food. In recent years, food trucks have become a legitimate dining option, **VENDING** a vast array of food and drink selections. Whether you want barbeque, crepes, gyros, Cajun, Asian, burgers, smoothies, or desserts, your local food truck vendors sell them all!

CHAPTER 9 REVIEW

Write the word from the Word Bank next to the correct definition. The answer key is on page 146.

Word Bank:

benefactor	choreographer	community	entourage
felon	indictment	nemesis	oppose
skeptical	tyrant		

1. _____ A unified body of individuals

2. _____ Criminal

3. _____ To disagree with or disapprove of

4. _____ Someone who helps another person by giving money

5. _____ Someone who uses power in a cruel and unfair way

6. _____ An accusation of a crime

7. _____ One's attendants or associates

8. _____ Enemy

9. _____ A person who creates dance sequences

10. _____ Relating to or having the characteristic of a doubter

CHAPTER 10

The Bridge to Core Vocabulary

This chapter focuses on bridging the vocabulary gap between middle school and high school. Included here are words that carry multiple meanings and words that will increasingly find their way into your academic work. They are the scaffolding for vocabulary success as you move into upper grades.

MULTIPLE MEANINGS

234 | ⭐ ALTERNATE

NOUN—A person who acts as a substitute
VERB—To interchange repeatedly or regularly; to rotate
ADJECTIVE—Interchanged repeatedly one for another

When a player gets injured, his **ALTERNATE**, or backup, comes into the game to take his place. When a team plays an opponent from their division, they **ALTERNATE** playing home and away games. Finally, beyond having a home and away uniform, many teams have an additional **ALTERNATE** uniform. These uniforms are typically a throwback to what was worn in previous eras.

235 | CAMOUFLAGE

NOUN—The act of obscuring things and blending in with the environment; a disguise
VERB—To hide using camoflauge

Nature photographers and biologists often must **CAMOUFLAGE** themselves when tracking animals. The need to remain hidden is very important because wild animals have a natural fear of humans. Without the use of **CAMOUFLAGE**, photographers would not be able to take the picture they want, and biologists would not be able to get close enough to the animals to gather important data.

236 | ★CONTENT

NOUN—Everything that is inside a container

NOUN—The chapters or divisions of a book

ADJECTIVE—Mentally or emotionally satisfied

> **PRO TIP**
>
> It is important to look beyond the obvious definition! Many words have multiple meanings. As you get into high school, it is often the secondary meaning that is used on tests or in books.

While cleaning out her classroom, the teacher found a bunch of old boxes in a storage closet. The **CONTENTS** of one of the boxes contained a variety of old history textbooks. A look at the table of **CONTENTS** revealed that the books were quite outdated. The last chapters focused on the Cold War between the U.S. and the U.S.S.R. The teacher decided that it was better to recycle the books than keep them or donate them. She felt **CONTENT** after cleaning the closet and reorganizing the classroom.

237 | ★DISCRIMINATE

VERB—To recognize the difference between things; to show preference; to differentiate

DISCRIMINATING

ADJECTIVE—A person having refined taste or good judgment

During the civil rights era, whites would **DISCRIMINATE** against blacks in many ways. Schools and other institutions would differentiate between white and black water fountains and bathrooms. Restaurants would often have a white entrance and a black entrance.

While **DISCRIMINATE** has a negative implication, you can also have **DISCRIMINATING** tastes. For example, someone with refined preferences might like independent films instead of huge blockbusters or pizza from a locally owned restaurant instead of a national chain like Domino's.

238 | ☆ ECLIPSE

NOUN—An obscuring of the light from one celestial body by the passage of another between it and the observer or between it and its source of illumination

VERB—To make less outstanding or important by comparison; to surpass

A lunar **ECLIPSE** is a really cool sight to see. In order to get a good view of the Earth's shadow passing in front of the moon, you need clear skies. A telescope is also a great tool for a more detailed view of the event. Lunar **ECLIPSES** occur two to four times a year.

Odell Beckham, Jr. had a record setting 2015 NFL season. Despite the feared curse of the Madden NFL game cover, Beckham Jr. had an amazing second year in the NFL. He **ECLIPSED** Randy Moss's record for the most receiving yards in a player's first two years in the NFL.

239 | ☆ ELABORATE

VERB—To add details in writing or speaking; to give additional or fuller detail

ADJECTIVE—Detailed and complicated in design and planning; complicated

Have you ever received a paper back from a teacher asking for more details? **ELABORATING** on supporting details in a paper or adding further analysis of a quote or passage is what teachers want from their students. The more **ELABORATE** the defense of a thesis or examination of a character, the more likely a student is to earn a high grade.

240 | ★FRICTION

*NOUN—Conflict between people or nations; **DISCORD** (Word 144)*
NOUN—Surface resistance to relative motion

The **FRICTION** between North Korea and South Korea has escalated in recent years. North Korea threatens South Korea regularly and tries to intimidate South Korea with missile launches and nuclear weapons capabilities.

If you need to build a fire without matches, locate some extremely dry wood and a stick. The idea is to create an ember using **FRICTION** between the wood and the stick. This method requires a lot of patience because it can take some time to rub and spin the stick on the dry wood before you get enough heat from the **FRICTION** to create a flame.

241 | GRAVE

NOUN—A place of burial for a dead body, typically a hole dug in the ground and marked by something
ADJECTIVE—Significantly serious; important

When a famous person dies, it is common that fans want to visit the **GRAVE** of the celebrity. The most famous example of this is Elvis Presley's **GRAVE** located at his *Graceland* estate in Memphis. Almost 40 years after his death, thousands of people visit *Graceland* every year and leave flowers and notes at Elvis's **GRAVE**.

The Fault in Our Stars tackles the **GRAVE** subject of childhood cancer. The main character, Hazel, has been battling thyroid cancer which has spread to her lungs. Despite this serious illness, Hazel does not give up on life. She is able to enjoy her friends, find her first boyfriend, and travel, all while fighting cancer.

242 | ★ PLOT

NOUN—A plan made in secret by a group of people to do something illegal or harmful

NOUN—The main events of a play, novel, movie, or similar work, devised and presented by the writer as an interrelated sequence

The **PLOT** of *Pretty Little Liars* centers on a missing girl, Alison, and the impact her disappearance has on her friends. The storyline is further complicated when the four remaining friends are accused of Alison's murder. What the friends know is that someone has hatched a **PLOT** to frame them for a murder they did not commit.

243 | ★ REVOLUTION

NOUN—An overthrow or repudiation and the thorough replacement of an established government or political system by the people governed

NOUN—A single orbit of one object around another or about an axis or center

In January of 2011, millions of protestors from all over Egypt took to the streets and city plazas to demonstrate against Egyptian President Hosni Mubarak. The peaceful demonstrations and marches turned violent; approximately 846 people were killed and over 6,000 were injured. Ultimately, the **REVOLUTION** was a success; Mubarak was removed from power, and Egypt held elections for a new president.

The earth completes one **REVOLUTION** on its axis every 24 hours, giving us day and night as we turn toward and away from the sun. The earth completes one **REVOLUTION** around the sun every 365.256 days, which is why we add one day to February every four years.

<table>
<tr><td colspan="3" align="center">KNOW YOUR ROOTS</td></tr>
<tr><td>LATIN ROOT:</td><td>EVOLVE</td><td>change over time</td></tr>
<tr><td rowspan="2">VOLV | twist; roll; turn</td><td>CONVOLUTED (DH Core)</td><td>very complicated</td></tr>
<tr><td>REVOLVE</td><td>to go around something</td></tr>
</table>

244 | ROOT

NOUN—The part of a plant that attaches it to the ground or to a support, typically underground, conveying water and nourishment to the rest of the plant via numerous branches and fibers

NOUN—The basic cause, source, or origin of something

The tree **ROOTS** were damaged by the flood. When that occurred, it weakened the tree's foundation. The flood was the **ROOT** of the problem and it was the reason the tree was so weak that it fell on the house.

245 | TREK

NOUN—A long walk or journey

VERB—To go on a long difficult journey

Sherpas lead hiking expeditions to mountain summits. They are highly trained and skilled climbers. Typically, several sherpas **TREK** ahead of a group of climbers to fix the path and carry gear while others follow behind in order to assist any climbers who are struggling. The work is dangerous, and **NUMEROUS** (Word 74) sherpas have died making the **TREK** to the summit of Mt. Everest.

KEY WORDS TO KNOW

246 | AUDIBLE

ADJECTIVE—Loud enough to be heard

Golf announcers are famous for being barely **AUDIBLE** on broadcasts. The announcers have to whisper because they are usually very close to the action. Golf requires a lot of concentration, and the slightest noise can be a distraction.

247 | ⭐ CULTURE

NOUN—The beliefs, customs, and arts of a particular society, group, place, or time

CULTURE shock can happen when a person travels from home to a different country. For example, the **CULTURE** in China is very different than in the U.S. China is a country ruled by a communist dictator. People in China have very few individual rights because community is valued over the individual. In the U.S., individual achievements and freedoms are celebrated, which is in contrast to the social norms in China. Additionally, the Chinese **REVERE** (Word 160) their elders and show them much respect. Senior citizens in America may be loved and respected by their families, but it is usually in a much more informal manner than in China. Experiencing a different **CULTURE** from your own may be challenging, but it can also be very rewarding!

248 | DOWNCAST

ADJECTIVE—A person feeling discouraged

After the chemistry review session, most of the class was **DOWNCAST**. The final exam was going to be harder than they expected, and it was clear it was going to require a lot more preparation in order to do well on the test.

249 | EVACUATE

VERB—To remove from a place; to vacate

Whether in a hurricane, flood, or wildfire, emergency personnel are responsible for assessing the danger and ordering citizens to vacate their homes and property. When people do not **EVACUATE** as ordered, they are risking their lives. It is essential in natural disasters to listen to the advice of law enforcement. If told to depart, residents should immediately follow the evacuation instructions.

250 | EXQUISITE

ADJECTIVE—Finely done or made; very beautiful or delicate

Adele is an **EXQUISITE** singer. Her beautiful voice propelled her to stardom. Music critics cite her powerful and emotional **TONES** (Word 57) as her greatest strength.

251 | FORLORN

ADJECTIVE—Feeling, condition, or appearance of being unhappy or miserable; pitiful

The abandoned kitten on the side of the road was very **FORLORN**. It was wet and muddy, giving it the appearance of a drowned rat. The kitten was also very skinny and shivering from the cold. The family had no choice but to rescue the pitiful kitten and take it home for some food, a bath, and a warm place to sleep.

252 | IMPLORE

VERB—To beg someone urgently

Have you ever wanted something so badly that you begged and begged your parents for it? Kids often **IMPLORE** their parents for the new *Call of Duty* game or the latest model of Beats headphones. Sometimes the strategy of begging works, but it can also backfire because parents don't want to give in to too many demands of their child.

253 | INTEGRITY

ADJECTIVE—The quality of being honest and moral

Martin Luther King, Jr. was a man of great **INTEGRITY**. Aside from his career as a Baptist minister, Dr. King was best known as a civil rights activist. He led non-violent protests against racial inequality and often had to face angry crowds. Despite their insults and violent attacks, Dr. King remained committed to his moral principles of non-violence and equality for all people until the day he died.

254 | MELANCHOLY

*ADJECTIVE—Sad; depressed; **FORLORN** (Word 251)*

It is not uncommon for people to get the wintertime blues. Cold weather, grey skies, and fewer hours of sunlight often leave people feeling **MELANCHOLY.** Sometimes a bright sunny day or the first flower blooming in early spring helps ease seasonal depression.

255 | OMINOUS

ADJECTIVE—Suggesting that something bad is going to happen in the future

Do you know the two indicators that a tornado may be coming? **OMINOUS**, black clouds begin to form, and the sky turns a strange shade of green. These are warning signs to take cover and consult your local news to get the latest weather report.

256 | PERVASIVE

ADJECTIVE—Spread throughout an area or a group of people

There are certain **PERVASIVE** smells that are unmistakable in cooking. Garlic and onion aromas spread throughout a house or restaurant and usually smell quite good. However, sometimes the overwhelming odor of fish lingers too long and can disperse far beyond the kitchen or the trash can, leaving a house really stinky!

257 | ⭐PREJUDICE

NOUN—A feeling of like or dislike for someone or something especially when it is illogical; **BIAS** *(Word 5)*

Lawyers and judges go to great lengths to pick a jury that doesn't have any **PREJUDICE** about the case. They survey potential jurors and ask them questions about their feelings and experiences. Any **BIAS** (Word 5) shown by a possible juror will usually excuse them from serving.

258 | SUCCINCT

NOUN—Briefly and clearly expressed

The older you get, the more important it is to be **SUCCINCT** with your words. This is true in writing and in speaking. Teachers appreciate it when students can express their thoughts clearly without using too many words. It is common for teachers to give writing assignments with a limit on pages or words as well as oral assignments with a time limit. It is a skill to be brief but thorough in expressive thought!

CHAPTER 10 REVIEW

Complete each word box. The answer key is on page 146.

Alternate:

Definition 1: _____

Definition 2: _____

Definition 3: _____

Content:

Definition 1: _____

Definition 2: _____

Definition 3: _____

Eclipse:

Definition in your own words: _____

_____

Definition in your own words: _____

_____

Elaborate:

Definition in your own words: _____

_____

Definition in your own words: _____

_____

Downcast:
List 3 synonyms: _____

Exquisite:
List 3 synonyms: _____

Implore:
List 3 synonyms: _____

Integrity:
List 3 synonyms: _____

Pervasive:
Use the word in a sentence that helps explain what it means.

_____

_____

Succinct:
Use the word in a sentence that helps explain what it means.

_____

_____

Fast Review

CHAPTER 1: ESSENTIAL 25 GREATEST HITS

1. **AUTHENTIC** *(adj.)*—Genuine; real; not false or copied

2. **BENEFIT** *(n.)*—Something that is advantageous or good
    BENEFIT *(v.)*—To help; to improve; to gain

3. **BENEVOLENT** *(adj.)*—Characterized by or expressing goodwill or kindly feelings; compassionate

4. **BELLIGERENT** *(adj.)*—Warlike; given to waging war; aggressively hostile

5. **BIAS** *(n.)*—An opinion that is preconceived or unreasoned; **PREJUDICE** (Word 257)

6. **COMPASSION** *(n.)*—A feeling of deep sympathy and sorrow for another who is stricken by misfortune, accompanied by a strong desire to alleviate the suffering

7. **COMPEL** *(v.)*—To drive; to force or submit

8. **CONFIDENTIAL** *(adj.)*—Spoken, written, or acted on in strict privacy or secrecy; secret

9. **DEBATE** *(n.)*—Discussion, argument, dispute
    DEBATE *(v.)*—To argue, discuss, deliberate, ponder, consider

10. **DYNAMIC** *(adj.)*—Pertaining to or characterized by energy or effective action; vigorously active or forceful; energetic

11. **ENDORSE** *(v.)*—To approve, support, or sustain
    ENDORSEMENT *(n.)*—An act of giving one's public approval or support to someone or something; recommendation

12. **FRUGAL** *(adj.)*—Economical in use or expenditure; prudently saving or sparing; not wasteful

13. **ILLUMINATE** *(v.)*—To supply or brighten with light; to light up; to make lucid or clear

14. **IRONY** *(n.)*—The use of words to convey a meaning that is the opposite of its literal meaning

15. **JEER** *(v.)*—To ridicule; to taunt; ; to mock

16. **LUCID** *(adj.)*—Clear-headed; rational; easily understood; completely intelligible or comprehensible

17. **MORTAL** *(adj.)*—Subject to dying; human; earthly

18. **NAÏVE** *(adj.)*—Innocent; unsophisticated; inexperienced

19. **NOVICE** *(n.)*—A beginner; someone who is not skilled

20. **RANCID** *(adj.)*—Rank, unpleasant, and stale; offensive or nasty; disagreeable

21. **REMINISCE** *(v.)*—To recall past experiences; to remember
    REMINISCENCE *(n.)*—The act or process of recalling past experiences or events; a mental impression retained and revived

22. **TACIT** *(adj.)*—Understood without being openly expressed; implied

23. **UNIQUE** *(adj.)*—Existing as the only one or as the sole example; single; unparalleled; incomparable

24. **VARIEGATED** *(adj.)*—Varied in appearance or color; diverse

25. **WRITHE** *(v.)*—To twist the body about or squirm, as in pain or violent effort

CHAPTER 2: LITERARY LANGUAGE

26. **ANALYZE** *(v.)*—To break down into parts and examine carefully

27. **ATTITUDE** *(n.)*—The way a person views something or tends to behave towards it; belief; mindset

28. **CHARACTERISTIC** *(n.)*—A trait; a feature

29. **CONCLUDE** *(v.)*—To bring to a close; to end
    CONCLUSION *(n.)*—The end; summation

30. **CONNOTE** *(v.)*—To prompt a reader to think about images and ideas beyond a word's literal meaning

31. **CONTEXTUALIZE** *(v.)*—To consider or provide information about the time, place, or circumstances of a story or event

32. **CONTRADICT** *(v.)*—To deny; present an opposing view

33. **CONTRAST** *(v.)*—To show differences between or among
    CONTRAST *(n.)*—Something that is different from something else

34. **DENOTE** *(v.)*—To indicate; to mean something; to show, mark, or be a sign of something

35. **FIGURATIVE** *(adj.)*—A form of language use in which writers and speakers convey something other than the exact meaning of their words; not **LITERAL** (Word 41)

36. **ILLOGICAL** *(adj.)*—Contrary or opposed to the fact

37. **INDICATE** *(v.)*—To be a sign of; show

38. **INFER** *(v.)*—To form an opinion from evidence, to reach a **CONCLUSION** (Word 29) based on known facts; to hint or suggest
    INFERENCE *(n.)*—A **CONCLUSION** (Word 29) or opinion reached on the basis of evidence and known facts; presumption

39. **INTERPRET** *(v.)*—To give or provide meaning of; explain; understand a message

40. **INVESTIGATE** *(v.)*—To examine thoroughly, as an idea; to probe; to inquire

41. **LITERAL** *(adj.)*—Completely true; factual; not **FIGURATIVE** (Word 35)

42. **OBJECTIVE** *(adj.)*—Open-minded; not influenced by personal feelings; not **SUBJECTIVE** (Word 52)

43. **OBSERVE** *(v.)*—To notice or see
    OBSERVATION *(n.)*—A statement or point of view based on what has been seen; an understanding based on first-hand evidence

44. **PERSPECTIVE** *(n.)*—Point of view, a way of looking at something

45. **PERSUADE** *(v.)*—To convince; bring around to one's way of thinking

46. **PLAUSIBLE** *(adj.)*—Believable or reasonable, given certain information to consider

47. **REFLECT** *(v.)*—To think about or consider

48. **RELEVANT** *(adj.)*—Related to the matter at hand; connected

49. **REQUISITE** *(adj.)*—Needed for a particular purpose

50. **RHETORIC** *(n.)*—Language that is intended to influence; eloquence

51. **SARCASTIC** *(adj.)*—The use of **IRONY** (Word 14) to mock or convey contempt

52. **SUBJECTIVE** *(adj.)*—Relating to one's own point of view; not **OBJECTIVE** (Word 42)

53. **SUMMARIZE** *(v.)*—To tell information again using fewer words
    SUMMARY *(n.)*—A brief statement that presents the main points in concise form

54. **SYMBOLIZE** *(v.)*—To stand for
    SYMBOL *(n.)*—A concrete object that represents an abstract idea
    SYMBOLIC *(adj.)*—Relating to or being used as a symbol; representative

55. **SYNTHESIZE** *(v.)*—To combine in order to make something new

56. **THEME** *(n.)*—A unifying idea that is a recurrent element in literary work or artistic work

57. **TONE** *(n.)*—A quality, feeling, or attitude expressed by the words that someone uses in speaking or writing

CHAPTER 3: WORDS THAT COUNT

58. **ACUTE** *(adj.)*—Intense; sharp; severe
    ACUTE *(adj.)*—An angle measuring less than 90 degrees

59. **AMORPHOUS** *(adj.)*—Without a clearly defined shape or form; vague

60. **COLOSSAL** *(adj.)*—Extraordinarily great in size; gigantic; huge

61. **CONCAVE** *(adj.)*—Curved inward like the interior of a circle; hollow and curved in

62. **CONGRUENT** *(adj.)*—Having identical shapes so that all parts correspond; agreeing; corresponding

63. **CONSECUTIVE** *(adj.)*—Following one another in uninterrupted succession or order; continuous

64. **CONVEX** *(adj.)*—Having a surface that is curved or rounded outward

65. **DEARTH** *(adj.)*—An inadequate supply; scarcity

66. **DEFICIENT** *(adj.)*—Insufficient, inadequate

67. **DILATION** *(n.)*—The widening or stretching of an opening

68. **EQUIVALENT** *(adj.)*—Equal in value, measure, force, effect, significance

69. **ESTIMATE** *(v.)*—To form an approximate judgment or opinion of something; evaluate

70. **FINITE** *(adj.)*—Having bounds or limits; restricted; not **INFINITE** (Word 72)

71. **IMMENSE** *(adj.)*—Vast; huge; very great

72. **INFINITE** *(adj.)*—Immeasurably great; endless; not **FINITE** (Word 70)

73. **NULL** *(adj.)*—Without value

74. **NUMEROUS** *(adj.)*—Very many; being or consisting in great quantity

75. **OBTUSE** *(adj.)*—Not quick or alert in perception; dull
                    An angle that measures greater than 90 degrees

76. **OUTLIER** *(n.)*—Something or someone that lies outside the main body or group; outcast

77. **PERIMETER** *(n.)*—The border or outer boundary

78. **PERPETUAL** *(adj.)*—Continuing or enduring forever; everlasting

79. **POLYMORPHOUS** *(adj.)*—Having, taking, or passing through many different forms or stages

80. **PROOF** *(n.)*—The evidence sufficient to establish something as true; demonstration

81. **REMOTE** *(adj.)*—Far apart; distant

82. **SCANT** *(adj.)*—Barely sufficient; inadequate

83. **SYMMETRY** *(n.)*—Similarity, correspondence, or a balance of systems or parts of a system

84. **VARIABLE** *(adj.)*—Likely to change; fluctuating

CHAPTER 4: PLANET EARTH

85. **ABYSS** *(n.)*—A deep immeasurable space; deep chasm

86. **AGRICULTURE** *(n.)*—The science or occupation of cultivating land; farming

87. **ALBINO** *(n.)*—An animal or plant with a marked deficiency of pigmentation

88. **ARID** *(adj.)*—Being without moisture; extremely dry; parched

89. **AZURE** *(adj.)*—Clear blue; serene

90. **BOUGH** *(n.)*—A branch of a tree

91. **BOUNDARY** *(n.)*—Something that indicates limits; border

92. **CONSTELLATION** *(n.)*—A group of stars that is known by a recognized name
    CONSTELLATION *(n.)*—A group or cluster of related things

93. **CONTAMINATE** *(v.)*—To make impure or unsuitable by contact or mixture with something unclean or bad; pollute

94. **CULTIVATE** *(v.)* — To grow and care for something; foster

95. **DILUTE** *(v.)*—To make thinner or weaker by the addition of water or a similar substance

96. **DOMESTIC** *(adj.)*—Of or relating to the home or homeland; native

97. **DROUGHT** *(n.)*—A period of dry weather; an extended shortage

98. **ERODE** *(v.)*—To eat into or away; to deteriorate

99. **EXCAVATE** *(v.)*—To remove by digging; dig out

100. **EXPLORE** *(v.)*—To examine; to investigate; probe

101. **FISSURE** *(n.)*—A long, narrow crack

102. **FLOURISH** *(v.)*—To be in a vigorous state; thrive

103. **HYBRID** *(adj.)*—Formed from two different elements or varieties

104. **INHABIT** *(v.)*—To live or dwell in a place; reside

105. **LUMINOUS** *(adj.)*—Emitting or reflecting steady, suffused, or glowing light; beaming

106. **PRECIPICE** *(n.)*—The steep face of a cliff

107. **TERRAIN** *(n.)*—A tract of land, especially with reference to its natural features

108. **TOIL** *(v.)*—To work under difficult and physically challenging conditions; to labor

109. **VISAGE** *(n.)*—The face

110. **WANE** *(v.)*—To decrease in strength and intensity

111. **ZENITH** *(n.)*—The highest point, peak

CHAPTER 5: ALL ABOUT ADJECTIVES

112. **ADEPT** *(adj.)*—Very skilled at something; expert

113. **AGILE** *(adj.)*—Able to move quickly and easily; deft

114. **AMIABLE** *(adj.)*—Friendly and pleasant; generally agreeable

115. **APATHETIC** *(adj.)*—Lacking interest or concern; indifferent

116. **ASTUTE** *(adj.)*—Mentally sharp or clever; smart

117. **BRASH** *(adj.)*—Confident and aggressive; bold

118. **COMPETENT** *(adj.)*—Having the necessary ability or skills

119. **CONGENIAL** *(adj.)*—Having the same nature, disposition, or tastes; agreeable

120. **CONVENTIONAL** *(adj.)*—Based on what is generally done or accepted; customary

121. **CORPULENT** *(adj.)*—Large or bulky; fat

122. **DEVOUT** *(adj.)*—Deeply religious

123. **DUBIOUS** *(adj.)*—Unsure or uncertain, feeling doubt about something

124. **EMACIATED** *(adj.)*—Abnormally thin

125. **EXUBERANT** *(adj.)*—Very happy, lively, or energetic; vivacious

126. **IMMACULATE** *(adj.)*—Perfectly clean; pristine

127. **INDIGNANT** *(adj.)*—Feeling or showing anger because of something that is unfair or wrong

128. **INTREPID** *(adj.)*—Very bold or brave; fearless

129. **JUBILANT** *(adj.)*—Feeling or expressing great joy; very happy

130. **MALICIOUS** *(adj.)*—Having or showing a desire to cause harm to someone; mean

131. **PUNY** *(adj.)*—Of less than normal size and strength; weak

132. **ROBUST** *(adj.)*—Strong and healthy

133. **TIMID** *(adj.)*—Demonstrating a lack of confidence; shy

134. **VERSATILE** *(adj.)*—Able to adapt to many different situations or activities; flexible

135. **VIGILANT** *(adj.)*—Keeping a careful watch

136. **ZEALOUS** *(adj.)*—Having or showing enthusiasm

CHAPTER 6: THIS DAY IN HISTORY

137. **ABDICATE** *(v.)*—To renounce or relinquish a throne, right, power, claim, or responsibility, especially in a formal manner

138. **AFFILIATION** *(n.)*—The state of being associated

139. **ANIMOSITY** *(n.)*—A feeling of strong dislike

140. **AUTHORITY** *(n.)*—The power or right to control, judge, or prohibit the actions of others

141. **BRANDISH** *(v.)*—To shake or wave something; to display

142. **CONTENTIOUS** *(adj.)*—Tending to strife; argumentative

143. **DECREE** *(n.)*—A formal or authoritative order

144. **DISCORD** *(n.)*—Conflict between people or nations; disagreement

145. **ENDEAVOR** *(v.)*—To exert oneself; strive

146. **ERADICATE** *(v.)*—To destroy completely; obliterate

147. **FOREBEAR** *(n.)*—An ancestor

148. **HYSTERIA** *(n.)*—An uncontrollable outburst of emotion or fear

149. **INGENUITY** *(adj.)*—The quality of being clever

150. **LOCOMOTION** *(n.)*—The power to move to one place or another

151. **MANDATE** *(v.)*—To order; to command
     MANDATE *(n.)*—An authoritative order or command

152. **PILFER** *(v.)*—To steal; thieve

153. **PLIGHT** *(n.)*—An unfortunate condition or state

154. **PRAGMATIC** *(adj.)*—Dealing with things sensibly; practical

155. **PRUDENT** *(adj.)*—Showing care and thought for the future; wise

156. **QUARANTINE** *(n.)*—A state of isolation
     QUARANTINE *(v.)*—imposed isolation

157. **RATIFY** *(v.)*—To approve

158. **RAZE** *(v.)*—Completely destroy; demolish

159. **RELINQUISH** *(v.)*—Voluntarily give up; renounce

160. **REVERE** *(v.)*—Feel deep respect for something
     REVERENCE *(n.)*—Deep respect for someone or something

161. **SEVER** *(v.)*—Divide by cutting or slicing; separate

162. **TURMOIL** *(n.)*—A state of great confusion and uncertainty; upheaval

163. **ZEAL** *(n.)*—A strong feeling of interest that makes someone very eager to do something; enthusiasm
     ZEALOT *(n.)*—A person who has very strong feelings about something; an extremist

CHAPTER 7: CELEBRITY SIGHTINGS

164. **ADMONISH** *(v.)*—To warn or caution against something; scold

165. **ALLEGE** *(v.)*—To claim or assert without proof; accuse

166. **APPREHENSIVE** *(adj.)*—Uneasy or fearful that something bad might happen; anxious

167. **CHIDE** *(v.)*—To scold

168. **CLICHÉ** *(n.)*—Anything that has become commonplace because of overuse; stereotype

169. **DEROGATORY** *(adj.)*—Showing a disrespectful attitude; insulting

170. **ECSTATIC** *(adj.)*—Full of joyful excitement; elated

171. **GARRULOUS** *(adj.)*—Very talkative; excessively chatty

172. **GAUDY** *(adj.)*—Extremely bright or showy; flashy

173. **GLUTTONY** *(n.)*—Habitual greed; excess

174. **IMITATION** *(n.)*— A copy of something or someone; impersonation
     IMITATE *(v.)*—To mimic or impersonate; copy

175. **INFAMOUS** *(adj.)*—Well known for a bad reputation; **NOTORIOUS** (Word 178)

176. **LAPEL** *(n.)*—One of the two folds of fabric that is below the collar on each side of a coat or jacket

177. **LAVISH** *(adj.)*—Luxurious; fancy

178. **NOTORIOUS** *(adj.)*—Famous for a bad reputation; **INFAMOUS** (Word 175)

179. **OPULENT** *(adj.)*—Very expensive; luxurious; grand

180. **OSTENTATIOUS** *(adj.)*—Characterized by an obvious show to impress others; **GAUDY** (Word 172)

181. **RANT** *(n.)*—A spell of ranting; tirade
RANT *(v.)*—To speak or shout in a wild way

182. **RAVE** *(n.)*—An enthusiastic review of something; praise
RAVE *(v.)*—To talk wildly
RAVE *(adj.)*—Enthusiastic

183. **RENDEZVOUS** *(n.)*—A meeting at an agreed time and place; appointment
RENDEZVOUS *(v.)*—To meet at an agreed time and place

184. **SHREWD** *(adj.)*—Having smart powers of judgment; intelligent

185. **TEDIOUS** *(adj.)*—Long and tiresome, boring; dull

186. **VERBOSE** *(adj.)*—Using more words than are needed; wordy; **GARRULOUS** (Word 171)

CHAPTER 8: SO THE STORY GOES

187. **ADORN** *(v.)*—To add beauty; to decorate

188. **AKIN** *(adj.)*—Of similar character; related

189. **BUNGALOW** *(n.)*—A small cottage

190. **CLING** *(v.)*—To hold tight

191. **COMATOSE** *(adj.)*—In a state of unconsciousness

192. **DAWDLE** *(v.)*—To waste time; linger

193. **DILAPIDATED** *(adj.)*—In a state of disrepair or ruin

194. **DURATION** *(n.)*—The length of time something lasts

195. **FALLIBLE** *(adj.)*—Capable of making mistakes; not accurate

196. **HAUGHTY** *(adj.)*—Arrogantly superior; conceited

197. **HINDER** *(v.)*—To create difficulties for something or someone; thwart

198. **HOVEL** *(n.)*—A small, very humble house

199. **INSOLENT** *(adj.)*—Showing an arrogant lack of respect; rude

200. **IRATE** *(adj.)*—Characterized by great anger; furious

201. **LAMENT** *(v.)*—To express deep sorrow; grieve

202. **LENIENT** *(adj.)*—Permissive; indulgent

203. **MEANDER** *(v.)*—To wander aimlessly

204. **OMEN** *(n.)*—An occurrence seen as sign of future happiness or disaster

205. **PATHETIC** *(adj.)*—Provoking pity; wretched

206. **PERPETRATOR** *(n.)*—A person who commits a crime

207. **PRECOCIOUS** *(adj.)*—A child having advanced mental development; mature

208. **PROCURE** *(v.)*—To obtain something

209. **PROPHESY** *(n.)*—A prediction

210. **RUE** *(v.)*—To bitterly regret

211. **SLOVENLY** *(adj.)*—Messy and dirty

212. **SURLY** *(adj.)*—Ill-tempered and unfriendly; sullen

213. **VILLAIN** *(n.)*—A character whose evil actions are central to the plot; **FELON** (Word 223)

214. **VINDICTIVE** *(adj.)*—Inclined to revenge; vengeful

CHAPTER 9: TASKMASTERS, TASKS, AND TOOLS

215. **BENEFACTOR** *(n.)*—Someone who helps another person or group by giving money; patron

216. **CHOREOGRAPHER** *(n.)*—A person who creates dance sequences, especially for stage and screen performances

217. **CLEAVER** *(n.)*—A tool with a heavy, broad blade.

218. **COLLABORATOR** *(n.)*—A person who works jointly with other people
COLLABORATE *(v.)*—To work jointly with others; cooperate

219. **COMMENTATOR** *(n.)*—A person who discusses important people or events

220. **COMMUNITY** *(n.)*—A unified body of individuals; neighborhood

221. **COUNSEL** *(n.)*—Advice given to someone
COUNSEL *(v.)*—To give advice to someone

222. **ENTOURAGE** *(n.)*—One's attendants or associates

223. **FELON** *(n.)*—One who has committed a felony; criminal

224. **GOURMAND** *(n.)*—Someone who enjoys good food, often to excess

225. **INCISION** *(n.)*—A surgical cut made into skin or flesh

226. **INDICTMENT** *(n.)*—A formal charge or accusation of a crime

227. **PROPOSE** *(v.)*—To put forward an idea or plan; suggest

228. **NEMESIS** *(n.)*—A rival or opponent that is difficult to defeat; enemy

229. **OPPOSITION** *(n.)*—A competitor or adversary; disagreement expressed through actions or words
OPPOSE *(v.)*—To disagree with or disapprove of; defy

230. **SKEPTIC** *(n.)*—A person inclined to question or doubt something accepted as factual; doubter
SKEPTICAL *(adj.)*—Relating to or having the characteristic of a doubter; disbelieving

231. **SURROGATE** *(n.)*—A substitute

232. **TYRANT** *(n.)*—Someone who uses power in a cruel and unfair way

233. **VEND** *(v.)*—sell something

CHAPTER 10: THE BRIDGE TO CORE VOCABULARY

234. **ALTERNATE** *(n.)*—A person who acts as a substitute
     ALTERNATE *(v.)*—To interchange repeatedly or regularly; rotate
     ALTERNATE *(adj.)*—Interchanged repeatedly one for another

235. **CAMOUFLAGE** *(n.)*— The act of obscuring things and blending
     in to the environment; a disguise
     CAMOUFLAGE *(v.)*— To hide or obscure by blending in to the
     environment

236. **CONTENT** *(n.)*—Everything that is inside a container
     CONTENT *(n.)*—The chapters or division of a book
     CONTENT *(adj.)*—Mentally or emotionally satisfied

237. **DISCRIMINATE** *(v.)*—To recognize the difference between
     things; to show preference; differentiate
     DISCRIMINATING *(adj.)*—A person having refined taste or good
     judgment

238. **ECLIPSE** *(n.)*—An obscuring of the light from one celestial
     body by the passage of another between it and the observer
     or between it and its source of illumination
     ECLIPSE *(v.)*—To make less outstanding or important by
     comparison; to surpass

239. **ELABORATE** *(v.)*—To add details in writing or speaking; to give
     additional or fuller detail
     ELABORATE *(adj.)*—Detailed and complicated in design and
     planning; complicated

240. **FRICTION** *(n.)*—Conflict between people or nations; **DISCORD**
     (Word 144)
     FRICTION *(n.)*—Surface resistance to relative motion

241. **GRAVE** *(n.)*—A place of burial for a dead body, typically a hole
     dug in the ground and marked by something
     GRAVE *(adj.)*—Significantly serious; important

242. **PLOT** *(n.)*—A plan made in secret by a group of people to do something illegal or harmful
    PLOT *(n.)*—The main events of a play, novel, movie, or similar work, devised and presented by the writer as an interrelated sequence

243. **REVOLUTION** *(n.)*—An overthrow or repudiation and the thorough replacement of an established government or political system by the people governed
    REVOLUTION *(n.)*—A single orbit of one object around another or about an axis or center

244. **ROOT** *(n.)*—The part of a plant that attaches it to the ground or to a support, typically underground, conveying water and nourishment to the rest of the plant via numerous branches and fibers
    ROOT *(n.)*—The basic cause, source, or origin of something

245. **TREK** *(n.)*—A long walk or journey
    TREK *(v.)*—To go on a long difficult journey

246. **AUDIBLE** *(adj.)*—Loud enough to be heard

247. **CULTURE** *(n.)*—The beliefs, customs, and arts of a particular society, group, place, or time

248. **DOWNCAST** *(adj.)*—A person feeling discouraged

249. **EVACUATE** *(v.)*—To remove from a place; to vacate

250. **EXQUISITE** *(adj.)*—Finely done or made; very beautiful or delicate

251. **FORLORN** *(adj.)*—Feeling, condition, or appearance of being unhappy or miserable; pitiful

252. **IMPLORE** *(v.)*—To beg someone urgently

253. **INTEGRITY** *(adj.)*—The quality of being honest and moral

254. **MELANCHOLY** *(adj.)*—A gloomy state of mind; depression

255. **OMINOUS** *(adj.)*—Suggesting that something bad is going to happen in the future

256. **PERVASIVE** *(adj.)*—Spread throughout an area or a group of people

257. **PREJUDICE** *(n.)*—A feeling of like or dislike for someone or something especially when it is **ILLOGICAL** (Word 36); **BIAS** (Word 5)

258. **SUCCINCT** *(n.)*—Briefly and clearly expressed

Answer Keys

CHAPTER 1

17, 18, 8, 14, 20

12, 4, 13, 5, 9

6, 19, 1, 2, 15

3, 11, 10, 16, 7

CHAPTER 2

1. attitude

2. analyze

3. plausible

4. conclusion

5. summary

6. tone

7. objective, subjective

8. investigate

9. relevant

10. contrast

CHAPTER 3

1. remote

2. congruent

3. equivalent

4. consecutive

5. outlier

6. variable

7. immense

8. amorphous

9. finite

10. dearth

CHAPTER 4

10, 18, 19, 14, 9

11, 6, 2, 20, 16

4, 3, 12, 5, 1

8, 17, 13, 7, 15

CHAPTER 5

Answers will vary. Refer back to the word and definition to check your work. When you draw a word, make sure the image is vivid and/or humorous so that you will remember it easily!

CHAPTER 6

1. authority
2. eradicate
3. ingenuity
4. mandate
5. ratify
6. discord
7. animosity
8. turmoil
9. prudent
10. hysteria

CHAPTER 7

Answers will vary. Refer back to the word and definition to check your work. When you draw a word, make sure the image is vivid and/or humorous so that you will remember it easily!

CHAPTER 8

1. precocious
2. bungalow
3. meandered
4. haughty
5. irate
6. perpetrator
7. lenient
8. omen
9. surly
10. comatose
11. adorn
12. villain

CHAPTER 9

1. community
2. felon
3. oppose
4. benefactor
5. tyrant
6. indictment
7. entourage
8. nemesis
9. choreographer
10. skeptical

CHAPTER 10

Alternate:
1. substitute
2. rotate
3. interchanged repeatedly

Content:
1. everything inside a container
2. chapters of a book
3. satisfied

Eclipse and Elaborate:
Answers will vary. Refer back to the word and definition to check your work.

Downcast:
Answers may vary, but these are recommended answers:
gloomy, depressed, dispirited

Exquisite:
Answers may vary, but these are recommended answers:
lovely, elegant, magnificent

Implore:
Answers may vary, but these are recommended answers:
ask, request, beseech

Integrity:
Answers may vary, but these are recommended answers:
honor, ethics, decency

Pervasive and Succinct:
Answers will vary. Refer back to the word and definition to check your work.

INDEX

CPSIA information can be obtained at www.ICGtesting.com
Printed in the USA
BVOW02s1336140316

439890BV00001B/1/P